BOOK 4 OF THE
ADULT LEARNER SERIES

JUDITH ANDREWS GREEN
DIRECTOR,
ADULT BASIC EDUCATION
MAINE SCHOOL DISTRICT #17

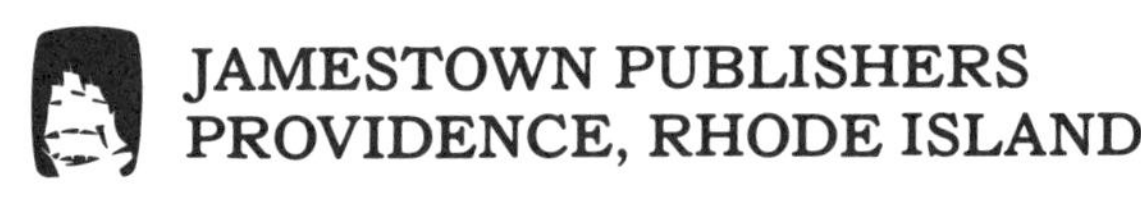

Catalog No. 203

Dr. Valdez

 Address all inquiries to Editor, Jamestown Publishers, Post Office Box 9168, Providence, Rhode Island 02940.

Cover Design by Stephen R. Anthony
Cover Illustration and
Story Illustrations by Janet Watt

Printed in the United States KI

86 87 88 89 90 6 5 4 3 2

ISBN 0-89061-211-0

Titles in This Series

No. 200, Murder by Radio
No. 201, The Man Who Stopped Time
No. 202, The Man with the Scar
No. 203, Dr. Valdez
No. 204, The Secret of Room 401
No. 205, A City for Ransom
No. 206, Nightmare Snow
No. 207, Peril on the Road
No. 208, Killer in a Trance?

For my father
with love

To the Reader

Ron Wells took the job with Dr. Valdez because he thought it would be fun.

And it *was* fun . . . until he found himself lost in the past—and then trapped in the future!

Travel with Ron into the land of the dinosaurs. Or travel to a world of flying cars, moving sidewalks, and buildings a mile high. Just climb into the time machine of Dr. Valdez. But be sure you can get back . . .

Before each chapter of the story, there are words for you to look at and learn. These words are in sentences so you can see how they will be used in the story. After each chapter there are questions for you to answer. These questions will give you an idea of how well you are reading.

Next come lessons that will help you to read, write and spell better. Other lessons tell you things you need to know about, and know how to do, to get along in life.

The answers to all the questions and exercises are in the back of the book. This lets you check your answers to see if they are right.

We hope you will like reading *Dr. Valdez* and learning all of the things this book teaches.

Contents

How to Use This Book

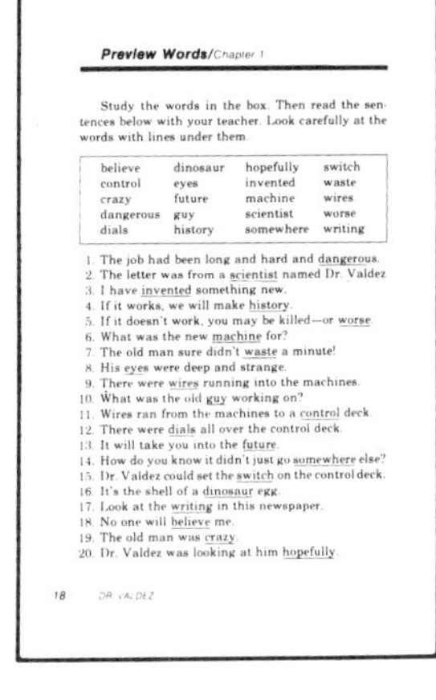

Preview Words/Chapter 1

Study the words in the box. Then read the sentences below with your teacher. Look carefully at the words with lines under them.

believe	dinosaur	hopefully	switch
control	eyes	invented	waste
crazy	future	machine	wires
dangerous	guy	scientist	worse
dials	history	somewhere	writing

1. The job had been long and hard and dangerous.
2. The letter was from a scientist named Dr. Valdez
3. I have invented something new.
4. If it works, we will make history.
5. If it doesn't work, you may be killed—or worse.
6. What was the new machine for?
7. The old man sure didn't waste a minute!
8. His eyes were deep and strange.
9. There were wires running into the machines.
10. What was the old guy working on?
11. Wires ran from the machines to a control deck.
12. There were dials all over the control deck.
13. It will take you into the future.
14. How do you know it didn't just go somewhere else?
15. Dr. Valdez could set the switch on the control deck.
16. It's the shell of a dinosaur egg.
17. Look at the writing in this newspaper.
18. No one will believe me.
19. The old man was crazy.
20. Dr. Valdez was looking at him hopefully.

18 DR. VALDEZ

1. Learn the Preview Words

Say the words in the box. Then read the sentences. Try to learn the words. See if you know what each sentence means.

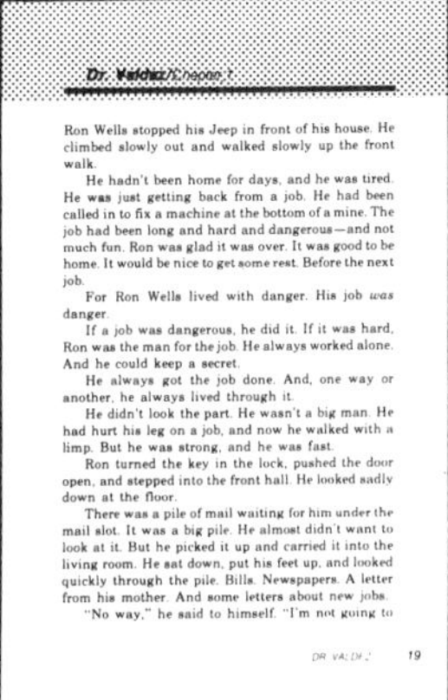

Dr. Valdez/Chapter 1

Ron Wells stopped his Jeep in front of his house. He climbed slowly out and walked slowly up the front walk.

He hadn't been home for days, and he was tired. He was just getting back from a job. He had been called in to fix a machine at the bottom of a mine. The job had been long and hard and dangerous—and not much fun. Ron was glad it was over. It was good to be home. It would be nice to get some rest. Before the next job.

For Ron Wells lived with danger. His job *was* danger.

If a job was dangerous, he did it. If it was hard, Ron was the man for the job. He always worked alone. And he could keep a secret.

He always got the job done. And, one way or another, he always lived through it.

He didn't look the part. He wasn't a big man. He had hurt his leg on a job, and now he walked with a limp. But he was strong, and he was fast.

Ron turned the key in the lock, pushed the door open, and stepped into the front hall. He looked sadly down at the floor.

There was a pile of mail waiting for him under the mail slot. It was a big pile. He almost didn't want to look at it. But he picked it up and carried it into the living room. He sat down, put his feet up, and looked quickly through the pile. Bills. Newspapers. A letter from his mother. And some letters about new jobs.

"No way," he said to himself. "I'm not going to

DR. VALDEZ 19

2. Read the Chapter

As you read, try to follow the story and what the people in it are doing. See what happens when Ron tests Dr. Valdez's time machine.

3. Answer: Comprehension Questions

Put an x in the box next to the best answer to each question. Read all ten questions first and answer the easy ones. Then go back and answer the hard ones.

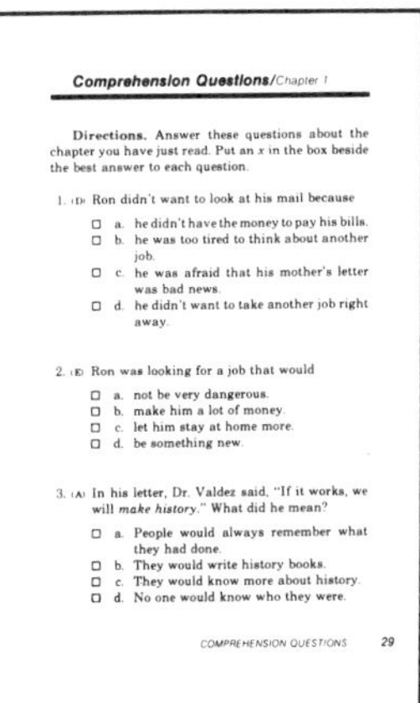

Comprehension Questions/Chapter 1

Directions. Answer these questions about the chapter you have just read. Put an x in the box beside the best answer to each question.

1. (D) Ron didn't want to look at his mail because
   - ☐ a. he didn't have the money to pay his bills.
   - ☐ b. he was too tired to think about another job.
   - ☐ c. he was afraid that his mother's letter was bad news.
   - ☐ d. he didn't want to take another job right away.

2. (E) Ron was looking for a job that would
   - ☐ a. not be very dangerous.
   - ☐ b. make him a lot of money.
   - ☐ c. let him stay at home more.
   - ☐ d. be something new.

3. (A) In his letter, Dr. Valdez said, "If it works, we will *make history*." What did he mean?
   - ☐ a. People would always remember what they had done.
   - ☐ b. They would write history books.
   - ☐ c. They would know more about history.
   - ☐ d. No one would know who they were.

COMPREHENSION QUESTIONS 29

4. Correct Your Answers

Use the Answer Key on page 204. If your answer is wrong, circle that box and put an *x* in the right box.

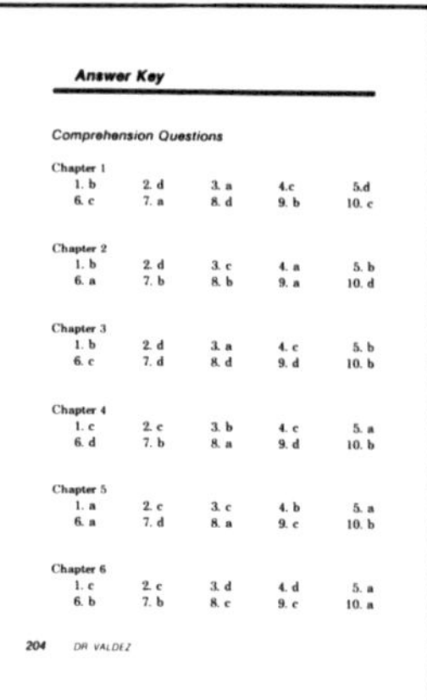

Answer Key

Comprehension Questions

Chapter 1

1. b	2. d	3. a	4.c	5.d
6. c	7. a	8. d	9. b	10. c

Chapter 2

1. b	2. d	3. c	4. a	5. b
6. a	7. b	8. b	9. a	10. d

Chapter 3

1. b	2. d	3. a	4. c	5. b
6. c	7. d	8. d	9. d	10. b

Chapter 4

1. c	2. c	3. b	4. c	5. a
6. d	7. b	8. a	9. d	10. b

Chapter 5

1. a	2. c	3. c	4. b	5. a
6. a	7. d	8. a	9. c	10. b

Chapter 6

1. c	2. c	3. d	4. d	5. a
6. b	7. b	8. c	9. c	10. a

204 DR VALDEZ

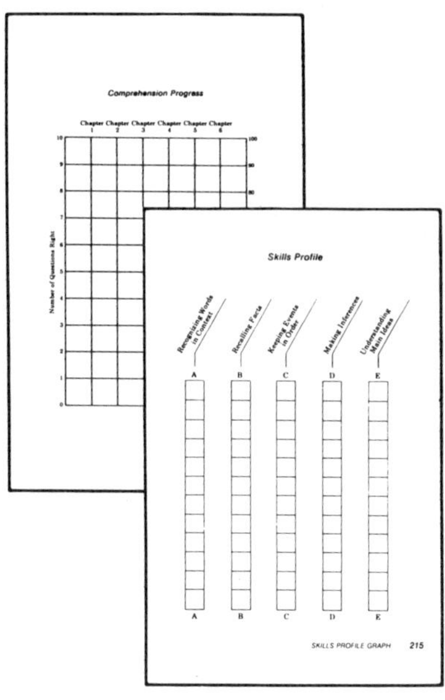

5. Fill in the Graphs

Fill in the graph on page 213 to show your comprehension score. Use the graph on page 215 to chart your skills.

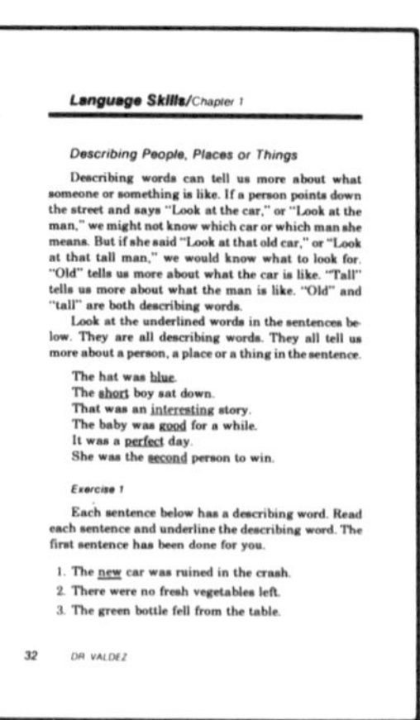

Language Skills/*Chapter 1*

Describing People, Places or Things

Describing words can tell us more about what someone or something is like. If a person points down the street and says "Look at the car," or "Look at the man," we might not know which car or which man she means. But if she said "Look at that old car," or "Look at that tall man," we would know what to look for. "Old" tells us more about what the car is like. "Tall" tells us more about what the man is like. "Old" and "tall" are both describing words.

Look at the underlined words in the sentences below. They are all describing words. They all tell us more about a person, a place or a thing in the sentence.

The hat was blue.
The short boy sat down.
That was an interesting story.
The baby was good for a while.
It was a perfect day.
She was the second person to win.

Exercise 1

Each sentence below has a describing word. Read each sentence and underline the describing word. The first sentence has been done for you.

1. The new car was ruined in the crash.
2. There were no fresh vegetables left.
3. The green bottle fell from the table.

32 DR VALDEZ

6. Read: Language Skills

This comes after the questions. Read the pages and do the exercises. Use the Answer Key on page 205 to correct the exercises.

7. *Read: Understanding Life Skills*

Read these pages and follow the step-by-step lessons. Use the Answer Key on page 209 to check your answers.

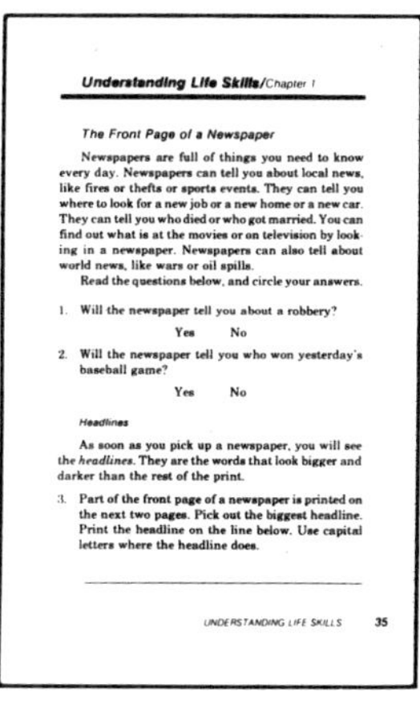

Understanding Life Skills/*Chapter 1*

The Front Page of a Newspaper

Newspapers are full of things you need to know every day. Newspapers can tell you about local news, like fires or thefts or sports events. They can tell you where to look for a new job or a new home or a new car. They can tell you who died or who got married. You can find out what is at the movies or on television by looking in a newspaper. Newspapers can also tell about world news, like wars or oil spills.

Read the questions below, and circle your answers.

1. Will the newspaper tell you about a robbery?

 Yes No

2. Will the newspaper tell you who won yesterday's baseball game?

 Yes No

Headlines

As soon as you pick up a newspaper, you will see the *headlines*. They are the words that look bigger and darker than the rest of the print.

3. Part of the front page of a newspaper is printed on the next two pages. Pick out the biggest headline. Print the headline on the line below. Use capital letters where the headline does.

____

UNDERSTANDING LIFE SKILLS 35

Applying Life Skills/*Chapter 1*

Reading the Front Page of a Newspaper

You know that every story in a newspaper has a *headline*. A headline tells in a few words what the whole story is about. Every headline is in print that is bigger and darker than the print of the story. The most important stories have the biggest headlines and take up the most space.

Exercise 1

The next page shows part of the front page of a newspaper. Use the front page to answer the questions below. Print your answers on the lines below the questions. Use capital letters where the newspaper does.

1. How many headlines are on the page? ________
2. How many stories are on the page? ________
3. How many columns are on the page? ________
4. Print the first four words of the most important headline. ________
5. Print the first five words of the caption of the photograph ________
6. Print the first three words of the headline that tells you about gas. ________

APPLYING LIFE SKILLS 41

8. *Practice: Applying Life Skills*

Read the instructions and do the Life Skills exercise. Take your time. Do the work carefully. Try to remember what you just read about understanding life skills. Use the Answer Key on page 210 to correct the exercise.

9. *Read the Chapter Again*

Go back to the story and read it once more. This time, as you read, try to feel all the interest and excitement the writer has built in.

Then, go on to the Preview Words for the next chapter.

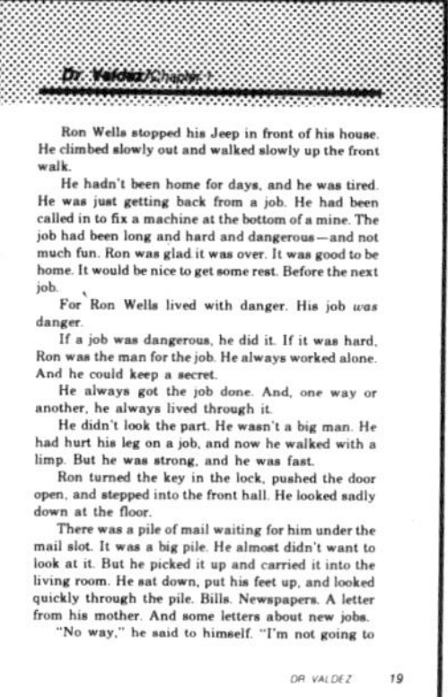

Dr. Valdez/*Chapter 1*

Ron Wells stopped his Jeep in front of his house. He climbed slowly out and walked slowly up the front walk.

He hadn't been home for days, and he was tired. He was just getting back from a job. He had been called in to fix a machine at the bottom of a mine. The job had been long and hard and dangerous—and not much fun. Ron was glad it was over. It was good to be home. It would be nice to get some rest. Before the next job.

For Ron Wells lived with danger. His job *was* danger.

If a job was dangerous, he did it. If it was hard, Ron was the man for the job. He always worked alone. And he could keep a secret.

He always got the job done. And, one way or another, he always lived through it.

He didn't look the part. He wasn't a big man. He had hurt his leg on a job, and now he walked with a limp. But he was strong, and he was fast.

Ron turned the key in the lock, pushed the door open, and stepped into the front hall. He looked sadly down at the floor.

There was a pile of mail waiting for him under the mail slot. It was a big pile. He almost didn't want to look at it. But he picked it up and carried it into the living room. He sat down, put his feet up, and looked quickly through the pile. Bills. Newspapers. A letter from his mother. And some letters about new jobs.

"No way," he said to himself. "I'm not going to

DR. VALDEZ 19

1

Dr. Valdez

Preview Words*/Chapter 1*

Study the words in the box. Then read the sentences below with your teacher. Look carefully at the words with lines under them.

believe	dinosaur	hopefully	switch
control	eyes	invented	waste
crazy	future	machine	wires
dangerous	guy	scientist	worse
dials	history	somewhere	writing

1. The job had been long and hard and dangerous.
2. The letter was from a scientist named Dr. Valdez.
3. I have invented something new.
4. If it works, we will make history.
5. If it doesn't work, you may be killed—or worse.
6. What was the new machine for?
7. The old man sure didn't waste a minute!
8. His eyes were deep and strange.
9. There were wires running into the machines.
10. What was the old guy working on?
11. Wires ran from the machines to a control deck.
12. There were dials all over the control deck.
13. It will take you into the future.
14. How do you know it didn't just go somewhere else?
15. Dr. Valdez could set the switch on the control deck.
16. It's the shell of a dinosaur egg.
17. Look at the writing in this newspaper.
18. No one will believe me.
19. The old man was crazy.
20. Dr. Valdez was looking at him hopefully.

Ron Wells stopped his Jeep in front of his house. He climbed slowly out and walked slowly up the front walk.

He hadn't been home for days, and he was tired. He was just getting back from a job. He had been called in to fix a machine at the bottom of a mine. The job had been long and hard and dangerous—and not much fun. Ron was glad it was over. It was good to be home. It would be nice to get some rest. Before the next job.

For Ron Wells lived with danger. His job *was* danger.

If a job was dangerous, he did it. If it was hard, Ron was the man for the job. He always worked alone. And he could keep a secret.

He always got the job done. And, one way or another, he always lived through it.

He didn't look the part. He wasn't a big man. He had hurt his leg on a job, and now he walked with a limp. But he was strong, and he was fast.

Ron turned the key in the lock, pushed the door open, and stepped into the front hall. He looked sadly down at the floor.

There was a pile of mail waiting for him under the mail slot. It was a big pile. He almost didn't want to look at it. But he picked it up and carried it into the living room. He sat down, put his feet up, and looked quickly through the pile. Bills. Newspapers. A letter from his mother. And some letters about new jobs.

"No way," he said to himself. "I'm not going to

look at these yet." He put the job letters to one side. He picked up his mother's letter.

But he couldn't help thinking about it. What job would he take next? Not one like the last one, that was for sure. He wanted something new. He wanted a job that would be fun for a change.

He picked up the job letters again. One letter looked good. It was from a scientist named Dr. Valdez. What kind of job would a scientist want him to do? Ron opened the letter and read it quickly. It said:

Dear Mr. Wells:

I need your help. I need someone to do a very dangerous job for me. I have been told that you are the man for the job.

I have invented a new machine. I need someone to test it. If it works, we will make history. We will make a lot of money, too. If it doesn't work, you may be killed—or worse.

If you think that you might want to take this job, call me at my lab. My phone number is 555-5113.

Thank you.

Yours,
Dr. H. J. Valdez

Ron read the letter again. This job looked good. It was something new, all right. It might even be fun.

The letter said that he would make history. And money, too. That sounded good. But what about this new machine? What was it? What did it do? If the machine didn't work, he might be killed. Well, he had been in danger before. He wasn't afraid of that. But the letter said that something even worse could happen. What? What was worse than getting killed?

He would have to find out. He would give Dr. Valdez a call. Who knows? This might be the job he was looking for.

It *had* to be better than the job in the mine.

Ron called the phone number. The phone rang and rang. At last someone picked it up. "Valdez here!" an old man said.

"This is Ron Wells," Ron said.

"Mr. Wells! Good!" said Dr. Valdez. "I'm glad you called! Do you think you might want the job?"

Ron smiled to himself. The old guy sure didn't waste a minute! "I'll have to know more about it," Ron told him. "What is this new machine? What does it do?"

"Oh, no, no! Not on the phone! I can't talk about it on the phone," Dr. Valdez said. "Why don't you come to my lab? We can talk about it here."

Ron went out to his Jeep. He got in and turned the key. "What am I doing?" he asked himself. "I just got home! I don't have to start a new job right now. I haven't even read my mother's letter! That Dr. Valdez must have really got to me. What's his big secret? I have to know what it's all about."

The lab was a long way from the city. It stood all by itself. The ground around it was very rocky. The lab looked lonely and strange.

When Ron drove up to the lab, Dr. Valdez was waiting for him by the door. He was old and bent over, with long white hair. His eyes were deep and strange.

Ron parked his Jeep next to the scientist's old Ford. Dr. Valdez shook his hand. Then he led him into the lab.

They walked through a big room. The room was full of machines with wires running into them. Ron didn't know what any of them were for. What was the old guy working on?

They walked past a cage with a monkey in it. Ron stopped to look at the monkey, but Dr. Valdez kept walking. Ron hurried after him.

They came to another door. Dr. Valdez stopped and looked at Ron. "Before we go in," he said, "you must give me your word. You must never tell what you will see here."

"You have my word," Ron said. "I can keep a secret."

Dr. Valdez looked at him for a long time. The old man's eyes seemed to cut right into him. Ron started to feel a bit strange. At last Dr. Valdez said, "All right." He unlocked the door and pushed it open. He walked through it, and Ron went after him.

They were in a room even bigger than the first one. At one end of the room was a set of machines. There were wires running from the machines to a big control deck. There were dials and switches all over it. More wires ran from the control deck to the other side of the room.

Ron looked to see where these wires went. They ran into something that looked like a phone booth. The booth was on runners that stuck up into the air. The booth stood all by itself at the end of the room.

"So this is the secret machine," Ron said. "Well, what does it do?"

"You will keep the secret even if you don't take the job?" Dr. Valdez asked.

"Yes, yes, I gave my word." Ron walked over to the control deck. "What *is* all this?" he asked. "I'm not a scientist. What do you want me to do? Do you want me to stand here when you turn it on and see if it blows up?"

"No, it won't blow up," Dr. Valdez said quickly. "This machine. . . ." He stopped talking. He stood looking at Ron.

Ron started to get mad. "Come on, old man, you know what I look like," he thought to himself. He put his hands in his pockets and walked around the control deck. "Well?" he said out loud.

"This machine will take you through time," Dr. Valdez said.

Ron stopped short. He turned to look at Dr. Valdez. "Through time? It's a time machine?" he asked.

"Yes, it is," Dr. Valdez said quietly.

"A time machine! It will take you through time? It will take you way back in the past? And into the future, too?" Ron asked. He shook his head. "Well, well, well. How does it work?" Suddenly Ron stopped and looked at Dr. Valdez. "Hey, wait a minute!" he said. "You want me to test this thing! That means you don't *know* if it works or not!"

Suddenly Ron felt cold. Dr. Valdez had said that he might be killed. Or worse.

He got hold of himself again. Why worry? This thing *couldn't* really work. When the old man started it up, it would just sit there and hum....

"It works," Dr. Valdez was saying. "I have tested it. I have sent the booth through time with no one in it. The booth has gone safely into the past and into the future. I even sent it through time with a monkey in it. And the monkey came back safely, too."

"How do you *know* the booth went through time? How do you know it didn't just go somewhere else?"

"Because it came back with things in it!" Dr. Valdez said. He pointed at a switch on the control deck. "I can set it so that the booth will stay in another time for a few days, or a few weeks. Then I bring it back. And sometimes there is something in it."

"Like what?"

"I sent it way back in the past, to the days of the dinosaurs. I left it there for quite a while. More than a year. When it came back, there was an eggshell in it."

"An eggshell?"

"Yes. It's over here." Dr. Valdez led Ron over to a case at one side of the room. "It's from a dinosaur egg."

Ron looked quickly at the shell. "It's not very big," he said. "I thought dinosaurs were really big."

"Not all of them. Some were quite small. And a big one couldn't get into the booth to lay an egg. But a small one might think the booth looked like a good place to hide."

Ron touched the shell. "But how do you *know* it's a dinosaur egg?" he asked.

"I took it to a friend of mine, another scientist. He studies dinosaurs. He said that it *looked* like a dinosaur egg. But he said it couldn't *be* one, because it was too new."

"Did you tell him about the time machine?" Ron asked. He could just see the old man telling a real scientist about the machine.

"No. I wasn't ready yet," Dr. Valdez said. "I don't want to tell anyone till I have proof that it works. I have to have proof that *everyone* will believe. My friend just said this must be some other kind of egg."

"I'll bet," Ron said to himself. To Dr. Valdez he said, "OK. What about the future? What do you have to show me from the future?"

"The booth came back from the future with a bit of newspaper. It's right here." Dr. Valdez pointed at a bit of paper next to the eggshell. Ron picked it up.

"The paper feels funny," Ron said. "It's so smooth and thin. Hey! Look at the writing! It looks like our writing, but . . . there's something funny about it! It doesn't look right."

"That's how our writing will look in the year 2481," Dr. Valdez said.

"In 500 years! How did you get this paper?" Ron asked.

"It must have blown into the booth in the wind. I sent the booth into the future with the door open. It came back with that in it."

Ron couldn't help it—he was starting to believe in it. "Why can't you use this as proof?" he asked. "This would show that the time machine works."

"No," Dr. Valdez said. "People would say it's a fake. Just like the egg shell. They won't believe me." He looked at Ron. "Do you believe me? You've got to! You've got to believe me!"

"Well,..." Ron said. "I don't know." What could he say? He couldn't take the job, of course. The old man was crazy, and the machine was nothing but a lot of wires.

Still, he hated to shoot the old man down. He felt kind of bad for the guy. Ron could see that he had put a lot of time and money into this machine. He might have been working on it for most of his life.

And wouldn't it be great if it did work! He would be the first person to travel through time! What a job *that* would be!

Dr. Valdez was looking at him hopefully. Ron started to shake his head. But before he could say anything, Dr. Valdez asked quickly, "Would you like to see it work? Would you like to see it travel through time? Of course, it takes a lot of power to make a trip. It costs $200 just to start up the machine. But maybe if you *saw* it work—then you would want to take the job!"

"Well, . . ." Ron said slowly. Why not? He might as well give the old guy a chance. "Yes, that would be good. I'd like to see it work."

"Good!" Dr. Valdez started to hurry over to the control deck. Then he stopped and looked at the booth. Then he looked at the clock on the wall. He took one more step. Then he stopped again.

Ron was watching him carefully. He didn't know what to think. What a crazy old man!

At last, Dr. Valdez came back to Ron. "You'll have to come back tomorrow," he said. "The machine just isn't ready for a run today. Come back tomorrow morning. I'll show it to you then. OK?"

Ron thought for a minute. "Yes. OK. Tomorrow morning. I'll be here." He turned and walked quickly out of the lab.

Out in the parking lot, he stopped. He felt as if he needed air. He leaned against his Jeep and looked back at the lab.

What was he going to do? He couldn't work for a crazy man! But was Dr. Valdez really crazy? Or did he really know what he was doing?

Well, he didn't have to start on another job right away. He could give the old man one more day to show him that the time machine would work. Right now, he would go home and read his mother's letter. And the rest of those job letters!

He climbed into his Jeep and started back to the city. As he drove, he began to smile to himself. A time machine! What a crazy thing! A *time machine!*

Comprehension Questions/*Chapter 1*

Directions. Answer these questions about the chapter you have just read. Put an *x* in the box beside the best answer to each question.

1. (D) Ron didn't want to look at his mail because

- ☐ a. he didn't have the money to pay his bills.
- ☐ b. he was too tired to think about another job.
- ☐ c. he was afraid that his mother's letter was bad news.
- ☐ d. he didn't want to take another job right away.

2. (E) Ron was looking for a job that would

- ☐ a. not be very dangerous.
- ☐ b. make him a lot of money.
- ☐ c. let him stay at home more.
- ☐ d. be something new.

3. (A) In his letter, Dr. Valdez said, "If it works, we will <u>make history</u>." What did he mean?

- ☐ a. People would always remember what they had done.
- ☐ b. They would write history books.
- ☐ c. They would know more about history.
- ☐ d. No one would know who they were.

4. (D) Why did Dr. Valdez keep looking at Ron?

- ☐ a. He thought he knew him from somewhere.
- ☐ b. He didn't believe he was really Ron Wells.
- ☐ c. He was afraid to tell anyone about the time machine.
- ☐ d. Ron kept saying strange things.

5. (C) When did Dr. Valdez tell Ron what he had invented?

- ☐ a. In his letter
- ☐ b. On the phone
- ☐ c. As soon as Ron got to the lab
- ☐ d. After he showed the machine to Ron

6. (B) What part of the machine made the trip through time?

- ☐ a. The control deck
- ☐ b. The dials
- ☐ c. The booth
- ☐ d. The lab

7. (B) What living thing had gone through time?

- ☐ a. The monkey
- ☐ b. Dr. Valdez
- ☐ c. A dinosaur
- ☐ d. A man from the future

8. (C) After Dr. Valdez showed Ron the dinosaur egg shell, he showed him

- ☐ a. a monkey in a cage.
- ☐ b. the control deck of the time machine.
- ☐ c. the booth of the time machine.
- ☐ d. a bit of newspaper.

9. (A) Ron didn't believe in the time machine, but he hated to shoot the old man down. What does this mean?

- ☐ a. He didn't want to kill Dr. Valdez.
- ☐ b. He didn't want to tell Dr. Valdez that he wouldn't test the time machine.
- ☐ c. He was afraid to shoot at the time machine because it might blow up.
- ☐ d. He hated that kind of job.

10. (E) Ron said that he would come back the next day mainly because

- ☐ a. he believed that the time machine would work.
- ☐ b. he thought Dr. Valdez would let him take a trip right away.
- ☐ c. he thought he should give Dr. Valdez a chance.
- ☐ d. he thought it would be funny if the time machine didn't work.

Skills Used to Answer Questions

A. Recognizing Words in Context
B. Recalling Facts
C. Keeping Events in Order
D. Making Inferences
E. Understanding Main Ideas

Describing People, Places or Things

Describing words can tell us more about what someone or something is like. If a person points down the street and says "Look at the car," or "Look at the man," we might not know which car or which man she means. But if she said "Look at that old car," or "Look at that tall man," we would know what to look for. "Old" tells us more about what the car is like. "Tall" tells us more about what the man is like. "Old" and "tall" are both describing words.

Look at the underlined words in the sentences below. They are all describing words. They all tell us more about a person, a place or a thing in the sentence.

The hat was blue.
The short boy sat down.
That was an interesting story.
The baby was good for a while.
It was a perfect day.
She was the second person to win.

Exercise 1

Each sentence below has a describing word. Read each sentence and underline the describing word. The first sentence has been done for you.

1. The new car was ruined in the crash.
2. There were no fresh vegetables left.
3. The green bottle fell from the table.

4. She thought the dress was pretty.
5. It was the third car to leave the yard.
6. She was the first woman to be mayor.
7. He enjoys good health.
8. She thought that the movie was dull.
9. Bad news is never welcomed.
10. He thought he was very clever.

Exercise 2

Look carefully at each pair of words below. One word of each pair is a describing word. It tells about the other word. Circle the describing word in each pair.

The example and the explanation that follow will help you.

Example: flower yellow

Explanation: Here is how to decide which word in this pair is the describing word. Try to use each word to describe the other word. Only one combination of words will make sense.

Ask yourself these questions. Can you have a flower yellow? Can you have a yellow flower? Only the second combination of the two words makes sense.

Answer: flower (yellow)

Yellow describes *flower*.

Now circle the describing word in each pair below.

1. round table
2. bird red
3. bowl large
4. empty box
5. hot stove

Describing words can make reading a story more fun. They add details that help us to see and feel more of what is happening. Describing words can bring a story to life.

Exercise 3

1. Read the sentences below. Think about the picture they make you see. How do they make you feel?

   The little boy walked down the long, dark street. It was a rainy night. He saw an old, empty house behind some dead trees on the corner. The house had many broken windows. He saw a strange animal look through one of them.

2. Go over the sentences again. Put an *x* through all the describing words.
3. Now read the sentences again. This time leave out all the words you have put an *x* through. Do you get the same picture as you did the first time you read the sentences?

The Front Page of a Newspaper

Newspapers are full of things you need to know every day. Newspapers can tell you about local news, like fires or thefts or sports events. They can tell you where to look for a new job or a new home or a new car. They can tell you who died or who got married. You can find out what is at the movies or on television by looking in a newspaper. Newspapers can also tell about world news, like wars or oil spills.

Read the questions below, and circle your answers.

1. Will the newspaper tell you about a robbery?

   Yes No

2. Will the newspaper tell you who won yesterday's baseball game?

   Yes No

Headlines

As soon as you pick up a newspaper, you will see the *headlines*. They are the words that look bigger and darker than the rest of the print.

3. Part of the front page of a newspaper is printed on the next two pages. Pick out the biggest headline. Print the headline on the line below. Use capital letters where the headline does.

   ____

Chicago Tribune

Midwest Edition

Bush Ends His GOP Race

After Iowa It Was All Downhill

By F. Richard Ciccone
Political editor
Chicago Tribune Press Service

HOUSTON—In the beginning, almost two years ago, it was George Bush's most sincere and often-stated belief that he would win the Republican presidential nomination, which he conceded Monday to Ronald Reagan.

For one brief night last January in a Des Moines hotel, many of his shouting supporters and several journalists shared that conviction. But his victory in the Iowa caucuses was only a high water mark for Bush and reflected more on his organizational skills than his ability to captivate the electorate in 1980.

He boasted in the final swing of his campaign last week that he was sur-

UPI Telephoto

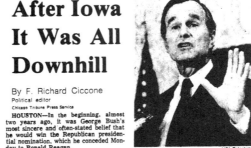

"I've never quit a fight in my life," said George Bush as he gave up on his GOP presidential quest Monday.

deserted him in New Hampshire.

He previewed his withdrawal last week by quoting a Kenny Rogers song, "You gotta know when to hold 'em, and know when to fold 'em."

But his favorite line was stolen from

Promises Support for Reagan

By F. Richard Ciccone
Political editor
Chicago Tribune Press Service

HOUSTON, TEX.—Former United Nations Ambassador George Bush withdrew Monday from the 1980 presidential campaign, leaving Ronald Reagan unchallenged for the Republican Party nomination that the former California governor has been seeking since 1968.

Bush repeated his denials of any interest in the GOP vice presidential nomination but left an opening for an invitation from Reagan by saying he would do everything possible to unite the Republican Party and help it win the presidency in November.

Bush, who also served as director of the Central Intelligence Agency, special envoy to China, and Texas congress-

AP Laserphoto

'Daddy's coming home'

The Navy band struck a chord and so did 15-month-old Marty Coppock as he waited for his dad and other crew members of the USS Nimitz. The carrier, from which the aborted Iranian hostage mission was launched, was to arrive on Monday in Norfolk, Va., from the Indian Ocean. Marty and hundreds of other families greeted three squadrons of aircraft that flew into Virginia Beach, Va., Sunday. Marty's dad, Lt. J. G. Skip Coppock, a pilot, was at sea for 143 days. President Carter flew to the Nimitz while it was still at sea. Story on Page 3.

that initially included Senators Howard Baker and Robert Dole, U.S. Reps. John Anderson and Philip Crane, and former Texas Gov. John Connally.

THE VICTORY in Iowa proved that Bush, more than any of the others, understood the primary process and had built an organization capable of competing with Reagan to the finish. It did not reveal that the candidate was not.

Bush, a Yale graduate who was born in New England and became a Texas millionaire, compiled a string of public and private successes that awed rather than impressed audiences. He seemed unable to develop an empathy with farmers, blue-collar workers, the elderly, and the poor who he needed to convert to his cause.

There also was a perception of arrogance in the speeches brimming with confidence based on a list of his personal achievements. It provided him with credibility when he was far down on the list of underdogs but became a disadvantage when he broke from the pack in Iowa and was thrust into public comparison with Reagan.

BUSH WAS PERHAPS the most accessible and urbane candidate who enjoyed describing his political fortunes in contemporary idioms. He found "Big Mo" in Iowa and treated momentum like a member of the family until it

ta, who explained why no one should count his team out until the game was ended by saying, "The opera ain't over until the fat lady sings."

Bush preached from the start that he needed a win in one of the early contests, and he got it in Iowa by winning a third of the 100,000 votes cast there. As the voter turnout grew larger in later contests, his organizational strength became less a factor than his personal appeal.

IOWA ALSO CREATED a raising of expectations that Bush could not fulfill.

His victory there pushed him into the lead in polls in New Hampshire, the initial testing ground of presidential candidates. It also may have lulled him into believing that he had prematurely achieved the one-on-one situation with Reagan that he had been seeking since the start of his campaign.

Although Reagan had a strong base in New Hampshire, and William Loeb, controversial publisher of the Manchester Union Leader, castigated Bush on the front page of his newspaper for days, Bush may have been his worst enemy by abetting those opponents who charged he was an elitist candidate.

Three days before the New Hampshire primary, Bush sat quietly, perhaps arrogantly, while Baker, Dole, and others still in the race were barred from a

Continued on page 6, col. 1

man, was the last of 10 men who initially challenged Reagan. They dropped out one by one as Reagan's primary and caucus victories gave him an insurmountable lead in delegates to the Republican National Convention.

"I'VE NEVER quit a fight in my life," Bush told a news conference after a weekend of deliberations at his Houston home.

"The reason I've continued to campaign is that I'd sincerely believed I had a chance of winning . . . I can be an optimist. But I also know how to count to 998," he said in reference to the number of delegates needed to secure the nomination, a total which Reagan already has surpassed. Bush said he sent a message congratulating Reagan and pledged his wholehearted support to helping Reagan and other Republicans win in the fall to "save the country from Jimmy Carter's weak, directionless, and incompetent leadership."

He said that although he would help delegates pledged to him win their elections in the remainder of the primaries and caucuses, he planned to attend the GOP convention in July and encourage his delegates to unite behind Reagan.

ASKED IF HIS strong showing in the highly populated states, combined with his pledge to help the party, would indi-

Continued on page 6, col. 1

Column 1

Israel Gets Tough Over West Bank

Violence in Hebron prompts crackdown

By Jonathan Broder

Tribune Map

Urges Council To Probe Meter Work

By Ronald Koziol

ALD. CLIFFORD Kelley [20th] said Monday he will call on the full Chicago City Council to urge the council's parking meter committee to resume its investigation of the city's parking meter inspection and repair program.

Kelley said disclosures Monday in The Tribune make it "imperative" that the committee actively pursue the investigation.

The Tribune disclosed that in the last three years, while the city paid $5.5 million to Duncan Traffic Equipment Co. for inspecting and repairing parking meters, it had to void 42,244 parking tickets written on cars parked at broken meters. Dismissing the tickets cost the city $295,008 in parking fine revenues.

The Tribune also disclosed that a spot check found many meters that remained broken for long periods. When a reporter found several vandalized meters at 63d Street and Marshfield Avenue in the last two weeks, a worker in the area said they had been broken since the first of the year.

KELLEY SAID that if it takes a council resolution to get the meter investigating committee moving again, he will introduce it at the next council meeting June 13.

The committee was set up a year ago at Kelley's request after The Tribune disclosed that the city had paid $270,000 to Duncan for inspecting parking meters in January and February of 1979 when most meters were buried in deep snow.

Since then, however, the committee has held only a few meetings. Ald. Wilson Frost [34th], committee chairman and a close ally of Mayor Byrne, has warned that a council investigation could interfere with a federal investigation of Duncan now under way.

"If we stop all city activities because of outside investigations, the mayor would have to hang a 'closed' sign outside her office door," Kelley said, alluding to the current Cook County grand jury inquiry of possible mob influence at City Hall.

"THE TRIBUNE disclosures raised some very critical points about the Duncan contract [to inspect and repair parking meters], and if the contract is

Continued on page 6, col 4

At the top of each story there will be a headline that tells in a few words what the whole story is about. You can tell by looking at the headline whether you are interested in reading the story or not.

4. Does every story have a headline? Circle your answer.

Yes No

The biggest headlines go with the most important stories. You will see the biggest headlines on the front page of the newspaper because that is where the most important news is.

Photographs

Another way of telling if you are interested in a story is by looking at the photograph that goes with it, if there is one. The photograph will show what the story is about.

5. Does every story have a photograph with it? Circle your answer.

Yes No

Look at the photographs on the sample front page. Underneath each photograph there is a short explanation. The explanation is called a *caption*. The caption explains what is going on in the picture.

Look at the caption under the small photograph on the sample front page. The caption tells you that this photograph is of George Bush. It says that George Bush will not run for President any more. You can tell that the story with this photograph would be about George Bush.

6. What is a caption? Circle your answer.

   A photograph

   A story that has a photograph

   An explanation of what is in a photograph

Columns

Newspapers are not printed just like books. You cannot read a newspaper by looking all the way from the left side of the page to the right side. Instead, a newspaper page is divided into columns that go up and down the page. Some columns go from the top of the page to the bottom.

Look again at the sample front page. You can see that the stories are printed in columns.

7. How many columns are there on this sample front page? Write the number on this line: ____________

Stories That Continue on Another Page

Sometimes a newspaper story will not fit on one page. It will be continued on another page. The words below the end of the first part of the story tell you where the rest of the story is.

You might be reading an article about auto thefts in your town. Page 1 might have only part of the story. Below the bottom of the last column you would see words like these:

See THEFTS, Page 17

These words tell you two things. They tell you to turn to page 17 for the rest of your story. And they tell you that THEFTS is the headline you will find on page 17.

When you turn to page 17, you will see these words:

Thefts

Continued from Page 1

These words let you know you have the right story. You have the second part of the story on auto thefts that started on page 1.

Reading the Front Page of a Newspaper

You know that every story in a newspaper has a *headline.* A headline tells in a few words what the whole story is about. Every headline is in print that is bigger and darker than the print of the story. The most important stories have the biggest headlines and take up the most space.

Exercise 1

The next two pages show part of the front page of a newspaper. Use the front page to answer the questions below. Print your answers on the lines below the questions. Use capital letters where the newspaper does.

1. How many headlines are on the page? ________
2. How many stories are on the page? ________
3. How many columns are on the page? ________
4. Print the first four words of the most important headline. ________________
5. Print the first five words of the caption of the photograph. ________________
6. Print the first three words of the headline that tells you about gas. ________________

The Boston Globe

WEATHER
FRIDAY — Mostly sunny, 80s
SATURDAY — Partly sunny, 80s
HIGH TIDE — 7:11 a.m., 7:46 p.m.
FULL REPORT — PAGE 71

NEWS ANALYSIS

The State of the Right Wing

'The left is old and tired. So many of their leaders have gone on, like Hubert Humphrey. They had a lot of successes and victories over 30 years, they got to be on the fat side, sluggish, not lean and hungry. We in the New Right are not yet running the show; it's the old Avis thing, we've got to try harder.'

— Richard Viguerie

'It just seems that over the years they (liberals) have not marshaled the technology to match us.'

— Ralph Galliano

'In part, that's the fault of the left. It's sort of a left default. We ought to be doing the same thing.'

— Joseph Rauh

Tree limbs covered with ash formed a stark backdrop as searchers moved into Mt. St. Helens area Wednesday. AP PHOTO

There'll Be Gas for Summer— Costly Gas

By Paul Feeney
Globe Staff

Massachusetts motorists will have plenty of gasoline for summer travel, but they will be paying more for it, according to the state's ranking energy official.

Massachusetts Energy Secretary Joseph F. Fitzpatrick said yesterday that despite ample supplies, he expects gasoline prices to rise 1½ to 2 cents a gallon per week, increasing prices to between $1.35 and $1.40 cents a gallon by July 4.

Gasoline prices could break $1.60 a gallon by the end of the year, Fitzpatrick added.

He attributed the immediate increase to recent price increases by some 10 members of the Organization

Globe Staff

WASHINGTON — The growth stock in American politics right now is the right wing.

As the liberal leaders of the past three decades have died, retired or lost influence, an emerging group of conservative political technicians and operatives has harnessed modern techniques and emotionally charged issues with an eye toward yanking the government toward the right.

Some experts in the field believe that the right modeled its current operations on examples initially laid down by the left.

Is the left far behind the right in terms of organization?

"That's astonishingly true," said Wes McCune, a liberal who runs a watchdog group called Group Research Inc. out of a Washington townhouse, where for 18 years he has chronicled the rise of right-wing groups and put out a monthly newsletter for subscribers.

"The right has overtly copied the left," McCune said. The conservative Center for the Survival of a Free Congress is "a mirror-image of the National Committee for an Effective Congress," a liberal group.

National Conservative Political Action Committee (NCPAC) is structured like COPE, the Committee on Political Education, the political arm of the AFL-CIO. And the Conservative Caucus is the right's version of Common Cause, the liberal citizens lobby, McCune said.

CONSERVATIVES, Page 12

The President Is Shocked

By Curtis Wilkie
Globe Staff

KELSO, Wash. — President Jimmy Carter toured the decimated foothills of Mt. St. Helens by helicopter yesterday and afterward called the scene "the worst thing I have ever seen."

He assured the people of the Pacific Northwest that the federal government would work with state and local officials to try to restore the area and predicted it would someday become a "tourist attraction that would equal the Grand Canyon."

He said tourists and scientists would come from "all over the world" to view the site of "one of the most remarkable and formidable natural phenomena . . . of all recorded time."

Carter appeared awed by the dimensions of the damage after a fleet of helicopters bobbed and weaved through the mountain gorges and above the valleys and ruined logging camps for more than an hour.

Poor visibility and snow flurries prevented the President from approaching the volcano's crater at the summit of Mt. St. Helens, which was shrouded in fog and clouds.

But there was devastation enough along the route he took, following the winding north fork of the Toutle River. For miles there was nothing but shattered timber, laid flat like so many matchsticks, covered with dark gray ash.

At a stop in the town of Kelso, where he visited an emergency center, Carter said: "Somebody said it looks like a moonscape, but the moon looks like a golf course compared to what's up there. It's horrible-looking."

Accompanied by a number of ranking Administration officials, members of Congress and Washington Gov. Dixy Lee Ray, Carter took off from Portland, Ore., in the rain and mist early yesterday morning for the 50-mile trip to the base of Mt. St. Helens, which erupted Sunday morning.

At first the only evidence of damage were rivers swollen with mud and running out of their natural courses. Then the lush stands of towering firs began to be tinged with ash.

CARTER, Page 6

Federal Reserve Eases Credit Curbs; Prime Keeps Falling

The Federal Reserve Board yesterday, responding to "improved economic conditions" and citing tumbling interest rates and a drop in consumer loans, moved to partially dismantle the credit controls it imposed March 14. President Jimmy Carter called the action "appropriate," and expressed hope that banks will promptly pass on the benefits to loan customers.

□

Two of the nation's largest banks — both in New York — cut their prime lending rates a full point to 15½ percent yesterday. The action by Chase Manhattan Bank and Bankers Trust Co. put the cost of loans for top-shelf business borrowers at the lowest level in three months. Stories on Page 41.

[There will be enough filling stations open in New England to alleviate any fears of running out of gas while on a motoring trip this holiday weekend. Page 71.]

Currently, gasoline prices in Massachusetts average $1.20.6 for regular, $1.26.3 for premium, $1.22.7 for unleaded, and $1.28.5 for unleaded premium.

Massachusetts gasoline prices are the lowest in New England, while New Hampshire's are the highest in the region.

Fitzpatrick said that within the last 10 days, Saudi Arabia, Iraq, Qatar, United Arab Emirates, Indonesia, Kuwait and Libya, raised their prices by $2 a barrel. Venezuela will increase its prices from $1 to $3.50, depending on the grade of oil. Algeria has announced an increase of $1 a barrel, and Mexico has announced a hike of $1.50. Nigeria is expected to announce a price increase in the near future.

While the Saudi increase was retroactive to April 1, most of the other increases are retroactive to May 1 or later.

Fitzpatrick said these price predictions do not take into consideration the additional 10 cents a gallon charge proposed by President Jimmy Carter as a conservation measure.

That fee was supposed to be imposed a week ago, but has been ruled unconstitutional by a federal district judge. If that decision is reversed by a higher court, the fee is still expected to meet stiff resistance in Congress.

GASOLINE, Page 71

Exercise 2

Read the headlines below.

Youth Nabbed In Hold-Up
Tax Break For Elderly
Storm Watch For South County
Bus Fares Go Up Next Month
Dodgers Down By 1
Mayor Found Guilty
Car Crash Kills Two

On each line print one of the headlines. Use capital letters where the newspaper does. Print the headline that you might want to read first if you were:

1. a sports fan

   ____

2. a resident of South County

   ____

3. a senior citizen

   ____

4. a person who used public transportation

   ____

Finding Stories Continuing on Other Pages

Sometimes news stories begin on one page and continue on another page. The words below the first part of the story tell you what page the rest of the story is on. And they tell you what headline to look for on that page.

Exercise 3

Answer the questions below. Print your answers on the lines after the questions.

1. If you saw the words ***See BUDGET, Page 7*** at the bottom of the first part of the story, on what page would you find the rest of the story? Page: ______
2. What headline would you look for on that page? Use capital letters where the newspaper does.

____

2

The Time Machine

Preview Words/*Chapter 2*

Study the words in the box. Then read the sentences below with your teacher. Look carefully at the words with lines under them.

B.C.	dried	Indians	second
blurred	easy	July	signed
calm	flashed	known	weakly
clothes	glowed	level	wonder
different	inches	questions	wrong

1. Ron jumped up and put on his clothes.
2. He must have known I might not come back.
3. Lights flashed on and off.
4. Dials glowed softly.
5. It's set to go back 5000 years, to the year 3021 B.C.
6 It just takes a split second.
7. It will go to July 2, 3021 B.C.
8. The ground wasn't always at the same level.
9. I know where it was at different times in the past.
10. He couldn't help asking more questions.
11. She studies the way the Indians lived around here.
12. At the same time, the booth blurred.
13. It's an ear of corn—but it's only three inches long!
14. The corn she found was all dried up.
15. I wonder what they thought when they came back.
16. On the outside, he was as calm as ever.
17. What if you're wrong about the ground level?
18. "$20,000?" he asked weakly.
19. I'm letting you off easy.
20. He signed the paper.

The next morning, Ron woke up slowly. He didn't feel like getting up. He lay in bed with his eyes shut, thinking.

What should he do? Should he call up Dr. Valdez and tell him to forget it? It would all be just a waste of time. And he would really be doing the old guy a good turn. The time machine wouldn't work, of course, and Dr. Valdez would feel bad.

But what if it did work...?

The old man should have a chance. Ron jumped up. In a few minutes, he had put on his clothes and grabbed something to eat. Quickly, before he could change his mind again, he jumped into his Jeep and headed for the lab.

As he pulled into the parking lot, he saw Dr. Valdez standing by the door of the lab. The old scientist smiled when he saw the Jeep. "He must have been worried. He must have known I might not come back," Ron thought. "It's a good thing I did."

As soon as he got out of his Jeep, Dr. Valdez took him by the arm. He pulled Ron into the lab, past the monkey cage, and into the big room. He pulled him right up to the control deck.

The machine was on. A loud humming sound filled the room. Lights flashed on and off. Dials glowed softly.

Dr. Valdez pulled Ron up to the first set of dials. "Look here," he said. "I've set it to go back 5000 years, to the year 3021 B.C. It will get there on July 2 at 2:06 P.M."

"You can set it right to the minute?" Ron asked.

"Of course," Dr. Valdez said. "I'll let it stay there all through the fall and winter. It will come back from the past on . . . ."

"Hey, wait a minute!" Ron said. "I don't want to wait around that long! I can't spend all fall and winter waiting for that thing to come back! I've got other jobs waiting for me!"

"No,no, wait! It just takes a split second!" Dr. Valdez said.

"It does?"

"Yes! When I throw the switch, the booth will go through time. Let's say I throw the switch at 9:00. The booth will go into the past at 9:00 today. It will travel to July 2, 3021 B.C. Then it will sit there all fall and winter. But when it comes back, it will come back to 9:00 today. Just a split second later. Do you see?"

"I think so," Ron said. He didn't see, but he didn't want to get the old man going again. He turned to look at the booth. It was sunk down into the floor. Just the top was sticking up out of the hole. "Hey! What happened to the booth?" he asked.

Dr. Valdez pulled Ron over to the booth. "I put it down on the runners."

"Why?"

"Well, the ground wasn't always at the same level. It used to be much lower. I have studied where the ground level was at different times in the past. When I want to send the booth through time, I move it on the runners. Then it is always sitting right on the ground, no matter what time I send it to."

"Oh."

Dr. Valdez pulled Ron over to the door of the lab.

He opened the door and pointed outside. "Look at the ground. See how rocky it is? I picked this spot for my lab very carefully. I picked this spot because it had always been open ground. The floor of the lab is right at the ground level of today."

Ron was tired of being pulled around. And he was getting tired of hearing the old man talk. But he couldn't help asking more questions. "How did you know where the ground level was 5000 years ago?"

"I asked another friend of mine. She's a scientist who studies the way the Indians lived around here, a long time ago. She told me how far down she had to dig to get down to their old houses." He pointed back at the booth. "That's how far she had to dig."

"Well, you seem to think of everything," Ron said.

Dr. Valdez smiled happily. "Thank you," he said.

Ron felt bad. The poor old guy really believed all this. He was going to feel really down when it didn't work. "We might as well get this over with," Ron said to himself. He walked over to the control deck. "How about starting the machine now?" he said out loud.

"All right!" Dr. Valdez hurried over to the controls. He looked at the clock. "9:00 it is!" He started turning switches. "Now, just as soon as the machine warms up. . . ." A red light at the top of the control deck lit up. "There we are. Now, just lean down and open the door of the booth. Yes, that's right. You see that there's nothing in the booth. All right, stand back. Watch the booth carefully. Ready?"

Ron stepped back. He stood where he could see the booth and Dr. Valdez at the same time. He didn't believe anything would happen. But in his line of work, he watched everything carefully. "Ready," he said.

Dr. Valdez looked up at the clock. He set two dials. Then he pushed a button. "Full power," he called. The humming sound got even louder. "5 . . . 4 . . . 3 . . . 2 . . . 1 . . . now!"

Ron saw Dr. Valdez throw a big switch under the red light. At the same time, the booth blurred. For a split second, Ron felt as if he could see right through it. But then the humming sound stopped, and the red light went out.

The booth was still there.

"It didn't move!" Ron said.

Dr. Valdez pushed a button. The booth moved up to the same level as the lab floor. "Look inside," Dr. Valdez said.

Ron looked through the open door into the booth. There was something in it!

Ron put his hand into the booth. He picked up

something and held it in his hand.

It was an ear of corn. A tiny ear of corn.

"Look at this thing!" Ron said. "It's an ear of corn—but it's only three inches long!" He looked into the booth. "There's a pile of them in here!"

Dr. Valdez came over and looked at the ear of corn. He took it and turned it over and over in his hand. "My friend told me about this," he said, "when I asked her about the ground level. She told me about digging up the old Indian houses. She said that sometimes she found corn in them. Tiny ears of corn. This is what corn looked like 5000 years ago. Over the years, scientists found out how to make it grow bigger."

"Really?"

"Yes. Wild corn was very small. My friend showed me some. But the corn she found was all dried up. This is new."

Ron looked into the booth. "But why is there a pile of it in here?"

"Some Indians must have found the booth. They must have been using it to store their corn for the winter. I wonder what they thought when they came back and saw that it was gone."

Ron looked at the ear of corn in his hand. He looked at Dr. Valdez. He looked at the booth. He looked at the control deck. Then he looked again at the tiny ear of corn.

Indians? 5000 years ago?

Then it was true!

The time machine worked!

Ron was shaking inside. He was really on to something here. What a job this would be! He would travel through time!

But on the outside, he was as calm as ever. He stood up and looked at Dr. Valdez. "Where did the machine go?"

"It didn't go anywhere. It stayed right here. As I said, it's only gone for a split second. It comes back so fast that it *looks* as if it's there right along. But you can see it travel if you watch closely. You saw it, didn't you?"

"Yes. I think so. I mean, I saw something. The booth blurred a bit. I could kind of see through it, just for a second there."

"That's right," Dr. Valdez said.

"OK. I saw it travel. But where did it *go*?" Ron asked.

"I told you. It didn't go anywhere."

Ron started to get mad. Why did Dr. Valdez always talk in circles? "So it *is* a fake?" he asked loudly.

"No, no," Dr. Valdez said quickly. "It didn't go anywhere. It was right here, only it was in 3021 B.C. That was long before the city was here. Maybe the Indians lived right here. If my friend dug down under the lab, she might find what's left of their houses."

"So the Indians were right here?" Ron asked. "The booth never moves?"

"No. Not through space. Just through time. So we don't see it move."

Ron put his hands in his pockets. He walked slowly around the lab. He looked at the machines. He looked at the control deck. He looked at the booth. He picked up another ear of corn and threw it up in the air. He was thinking hard. Dr. Valdez just watched him.

"Dr. Valdez," Ron called from across the room. "Let's say I do make a trip. What if you send the booth into the past, and you're wrong about the ground level? Or what if you send the booth into the future, and there's a house there? What will happen?"

Dr. Valdez looked at Ron for a moment before he said anything. "I don't know," he said quietly.

"You don't know! You don't know what would happen! Now I know why you don't want to test it yourself!" Ron said.

Dr. Valdez just looked at him. "I have to be here in case something goes wrong," he said. "No one else would know as much as I do about the control deck."

Ron walked around the lab one more time. "You said the monkey made the trip OK?"

"Two times."

Ron walked over to the door. He stood and looked out. Dr. Valdez hurried after him. "Do you have any more questions?" the scientist asked.

Ron looked at him. The old man was strange. But Ron knew, after all those jobs, when to believe in someone. And somehow he believed in Dr. Valdez. "No," he said. "No more questions. I'll take the job."

"You will? Really? That's great!" Dr. Valdez shouted. He grabbed Ron's hand and shook it up and down. "That's great!"

Ron got his hand free and put it back in his pocket. "When do you want me to make the first trip?" he asked.

"Tomorrow? Would tomorrow be all right?"

"OK. Tomorrow it is. You be thinking what kind of proof you want me to bring back. Now, what about the money?"

"The money?"

"Yes, the money." Ron took a paper out of his pocket and gave it to Dr. Valdez. "The way I see it, I'll be doing two tests. One to the past, and one to the future. I'll want $20,000 for the first test."

Dr. Valdez dropped the paper as if he had been burned. "$20,000?" he asked weakly, holding onto the control deck.

"I'm letting you off easy. I like the job."

"But $20,000!"

"That's for the first test. If that goes OK, then I'll do the next test for less. Let's say $10,000."

"But . . . So much money! Just to test it!" Dr. Valdez said.

"So test it yourself!" Ron snapped.

Dr. Valdez picked up the paper and looked at it again. "It's a deal," he said at last. He signed the paper and gave it back to Ron.

Ron signed the paper, then put it back in his pocket. "See you tomorrow. 9:00 sharp," he said. Dr.

Valdez just waved his hand weakly.

Ron walked out of the lab. He felt better right away. It would be a good job. It would be fun. He did believe the old man. But he sure didn't have to hang around with him!

Quickly, Ron jumped into his Jeep and drove away.

Comprehension Questions/*Chapter 2*

Directions. Answer these questions about the chapter you have just read. Put an *x* in the box beside the best answer to each question.

1. (A) Ron thought of calling up Dr. Valdez and telling him to forget it. What did Ron mean?

   ☐ a. Dr. Valdez couldn't remember who Ron was.
   ☐ b. Ron didn't want to work for Dr. Valdez.
   ☐ c. Ron didn't remember Dr. Valdez's phone number.
   ☐ d. Dr. Valdez forgot how to work the time machine.

2. (B) Why was the booth on runners?

   ☐ a. Sometimes the lab was full of water.
   ☐ b. Dr. Valdez had to move the control deck.
   ☐ c. The lab was too low in the ground.
   ☐ d. The ground was lower in the past.

3. (B) How did Dr. Valdez know where the ground level was 5000 years ago?

   ☐ a. He went back in his time machine and looked.
   ☐ b. He asked the Indians who lived there.
   ☐ c. He asked a scientist who studied the Indians who used to live there.
   ☐ d. He asked a scientist who studied the dinosaurs who lived there.

4. (C) What happened after Dr. Valdez threw the big switch under the red light?

- ☐ a. The booth blurred.
- ☐ b. The whole lab shook.
- ☐ c. The lab went dark.
- ☐ d. The red light went on.

5. (A) In the past, Indians were using the booth to <u>store</u> their corn. What does this mean?

- ☐ a. They used it as a place to sell their corn.
- ☐ b. They used it as a place to keep their corn.
- ☐ c. They used it as a place to grow their corn.
- ☐ d. They used it to make their corn grow bigger.

6. (E) Why was it a good thing for Dr. Valdez that the booth came back with the Indian corn in it?

- ☐ a. The corn made Ron believe that the time machine worked.
- ☐ b. Dr. Valdez didn't have anything to eat.
- ☐ c. The corn kept the booth from falling over.
- ☐ d. Ron wanted to find more Indian corn.

7. (E) Ron asked Dr. Valdez what would happen if he was wrong about the time machine. What did Dr. Valdez say?

- ☐ a. Dr. Valdez didn't know what would happen.
- ☐ b. The control deck would blow up.
- ☐ c. The booth would bring Ron back safely.
- ☐ d. The booth would come back without Ron.

8. (D) Dr. Valdez thought that Ron was asking for too much money. But he signed the paper anyway. Why?

- ☐ a. Ron made him do it.
- ☐ b. There was no one else to test it.
- ☐ c. He had lots of money.
- ☐ d. He wanted to help Ron.

9. (C) What happened after Dr. Valdez signed the paper?

- ☐ a. Ron left quickly.
- ☐ b. Ron asked Dr. Valdez some more questions about the time machine.
- ☐ c. Dr. Valdez showed Ron how the time machine worked.
- ☐ d. Dr. Valdez changed his mind.

10. (D) How did Ron feel about Dr. Valdez when he left the lab?

- ☐ a. He thought he was very funny.
- ☐ b. He didn't think that he could keep a secret.
- ☐ c. He liked him, but he didn't believe him.
- ☐ d. He believed him, but he didn't like him.

Skills Used to Answer Questions

A. Recognizing Words in Context B. Recalling Facts
C. Keeping Events in Order D. Making Inferences
E. Understanding Main Ideas

Describing Actions

You know that some describing words tell us more about people, places or things. They say what someone or something is like.

There is another kind of describing word. It tells about actions. This kind of describing word says how something is done.

Look at the words that are underlined in the sentences below. All the underlined words say how something in the sentence was done. They all describe an action.

Sue ran quickly around the bases.

The bird woke me when it sang loudly.

Ted shut the door angrily.

In the first example, "quickly" tells how Sue ran around the bases. In the second example, "loudly" tells how the bird sang. In the third example, "angrily" tells how Ted shut the door. All these words describe actions in the sentence. They tell how something was done.

Most words that describe actions are easy to see. Words that describe actions usually end with *-ly*. This shows that the words tell about how something was done. Here are some examples.

-ly *Endings*

softly	swiftly	awfully
gladly	quietly	usually
cheerfully	fearfully	slowly

Exercise 1

Underline the words that describe actions in the sentences below. Remember that these words usually end in *-ly*. The first one has been done for you.

1. The children ran noisily through the room.
2. She spoke sadly of her past.
3. They did their jobs faithfully.
4. She smiled cheerfully at him.
5. The old man moved slowly to the door.
6. The little girl danced prettily across the room.
7. The class listened quietly to the record.
8. He looked nervously at the door.
9. The boat sailed smoothly across the water.
10. He glanced fearfully at the big dog.

Exercise 2

Look carefully at each pair of words on the next page. One word of each pair is a describing word. It tells about the other word. Circle the describing word in each pair.

The example and the explanation that follow will help you.

Example: sadly cry

Explanation: Here is how to decide which word in this pair is the describing word. Try to use each word to describe the other word. Only one combination of words will make sense.

Ask yourself these questions. Can you sadly cry? Can you cry sadly? Only the second combination of the two words makes sense.

Answer: sadly cry. *Sadly* describes *cry.*

Now circle the describing word in each pair below.

1. write clearly
2. carefully drive
3. talk seriously
4. skip lightly
5. silently sleep

Words that describe actions can make reading a story more fun. They help us to see and feel how things are being done. Words that describe actions can bring a story to life.

Exercise 3

1. Read the sentences below. Think about the picture they make you see. How do they make you feel?

   Tim looked playfully at Pat. She sat calmly reading a book. She clearly did not see him. He watched her cheerfully, waiting for her to look up. She read on steadily. Slowly and quietly Tim rose from his chair. He walked silently across the room to where Pat was sitting. He stopped carefully in back of her chair. Suddenly he took her book and said loudly, "Surprise!"

2. Go over the sentences again. Put an *x* through all the describing words.

3. Now read the sentences again. This time leave out all the words you have put an *x* through. Do you get the same picture as you did the first time you read the sentences?

Sections of a Newspaper

You know that there are many different kinds of stories in a newspaper. These stories are divided into *sections*, or parts, of the paper, according to what they are about. Each section has a different kind of story. For example, news stories are in the first section or two of the paper.

The sports stories are in a different section from the news stories. Three other important sections are Editorials, Amusements and Television. Having different kinds of stories in different sections of the newspaper makes it easier to find the stories you want to read.

1. Will a news story be in the same section of the paper as a story about cooking? Circle your answer.

   Yes No

The most important stories in any section are on the first pages of the section. The less important stories are on the next pages, and the least important stories are near the end of the section.

Editorials

Editorials tell the opinions of the editors, the people who run the newspaper. Editorials are not like news stories. They do not tell facts the way news stories do. Instead, editorials tell the points of view of the people who wrote them. You can agree or disagree with an editorial because it gives an opinion.

Read the two sentences below. Print the word "news" on the line after the sentence that tells a fact. Print the word "editorial" after the sentence that tells an opinion.

2. a. At 9:15 this morning, the First National Bank was robbed by two armed men.

   ____

   b. We think that the mayor has made a mistake in running for re-election.

   ____

Amusements and Television

Newspapers tell you things you can do for fun. The Amusements section tells you what is playing at the movies, what music you can hear, and where you can go to eat. Many papers have a longer Amusements section at the end of the week to tell you about things you can do that weekend.

The Television section lists all the programs you can get in your area. It gives the times and the channels for the programs.

The Amusements section can help you pick a restaurant to eat in. The ads from restaurants tell you important information about these eating places. An ad tells you the name, address and phone number of a restaurant. It tells you what days and hours the restaurant is open. An ad also tells you what kind of food and drinks the restaurant serves. And it tells you about how much money a meal will cost.

Answer the questions below, using information in the sentences you have just read. Circle your answers.

3. Will a restaurant ad tell you where the restaurant is?

Yes No

4. Will a restaurant ad tell you when the restaurant is open?

Yes No

Sports

Near the end of every paper there is a section on sports. The sports section has all the scores of the day's sports events. There also are stories about the most important games and players.

Sports sections also have charts to help tell how different teams and players are doing. One chart, called "Baseball Standings," appears below. It tells how each team is ranked in the Eastern Division of the American League.

BASEBALL STANDINGS
American League
Eastern Division

	W	L
New York	26	16
Milwaukee	22	19
Toronto	22	19
Boston	21	22
Cleveland	20	22
Baltimore	20	24
Detroit	18	24

The teams are listed in order according to how well they played. The team that has won the most games is first on the list. The team that has won the least games is last on the list.

Use this information to answer the questions below. Print your answers on the lines after each question.

5. Which team has won the most games?

____

6. Which team has won the least games?

____

If you look to the right of the list of teams you will find two columns of numbers. The first column starts with the letter *W*. This letter stands for games *won*. The numbers under the *W* tell you how many games the teams won.

The second column at the right of the list starts with the letter *L*. This tells you how many games the teams *lost*.

Almost every newspaper has all these different sections. Most newspapers have other sections as well. The best way of reading a newspaper is to choose one that you like and look at it often. That way you will get to know what sections are in your newspaper and where to find them.

Using the Sections of a Newspaper

You have just read about these newspaper sections: News, Editorials, Amusements, Television and Sports. Exercise 1 names different kinds of information you can find in a newspaper. Each kind of information is found in one of the sections you have learned about.

Exercise 1

Decide which section of the newspaper you would look in to find each kind of information listed below. Print the name of that section on the line below the information. Use a capital letter to begin the name of each section.

1. The score of yesterday's baseball game

   ____

2. An oil spill in the North Sea

   ____

3. An opinion about who you should vote for

   ____

4. The time the movie starts at the local theater

   ____

5. A fire in an old warehouse

---

6. The most valuable player in the National Basketball Association

---

Reading Baseball Standings

The chart below gives the baseball standings for the Western Division of the American League. Remember that the teams are listed by how well they have played. The team that has won the most games is listed first, and the team that has won the fewest games is listed last. The column headed by *W* tells you the number of games a team has won. The column headed by *L* tells you the number of games a team has lost.

BASEBALL STANDINGS
American League
Western Division

	W	L
Kansas City	25	18
Chicago	24	21
Oakland	23	21
Texas	22	21
Seattle	22	23
California.............	18	24
Minnesota	18	27

Exercise 2

Use the chart to answer the questions below. Print your answers on the lines below each question.

1. What team is first in this division?

   ____

2. How many games has Chicago won?

   ____

3. How many games has Chicago lost?

   ____

4. What team is last in this division?

   ____

5. How many games has the team in last place won?

   ____

3

Into the Past

Preview Words/*Chapter 3*

Study the words in the box. Then read the sentences below with your teacher. Look carefully at the words with lines under them.

between	ferns	jungle	pictures
breath	guess	knife	remember
coffee	hacked	leaves	shadow
country	handle	meant	splashing
enough	idea	mountains	swamps

1. That sounds like a good idea.
2. All of the country was low ground.
3. There were a lot of swamps.
4. Then the tall mountains were pushed up.
5. Let's have a cup of coffee.
6. Dr. Valdez showed Ron some pictures.
7. You just want me to bring you some leaves?
8. The look like ferns to me.
9. You can cut down some leaves with this knife.
10. Do you think you can handle it?
11. I've used one of these in the jungle.
12. Just remember—you have ten hours.
13. I guess the machine didn't work.
14. The knife wasn't meant for cutting a hole.
15. He could hear dinosaurs splashing in the water.
16. He got up and put the knife between his teeth.
17. He hacked at the bottom of the fern.
18. The huge shadow came across the grass.
19. He couldn't lift himself high enough to hit them.
20. Ron stood still, trying to catch his breath.

The next morning was cold and rainy. Ron ran out of his house and jumped into his Jeep. He pulled out into the street. It was raining so hard that he could hardly see where he was going. He had to take it slow all the way to the lab.

He pulled into the lab parking lot at 9:00. The old Ford was in the same spot. "I'll bet Dr. Valdez has been here for a long time already," Ron thought. "The old boy must want to get this test over with." He jumped out of the Jeep and ran into the lab.

The front door was open for him. He walked into the first room. He stopped and looked around. No one was there. But he could hear a loud humming sound. It was coming from the next room, where the time machine was.

He walked across the room to the other door. He tried to open it, but it was locked. He knocked on the door. No one came. "He can't hear me with that machine running," Ron thought. He banged on the door with his hand. Suddenly the humming sound died down. He could hear footsteps coming across the room. The door popped open, and Dr. Valdez was looking at him.

The old scientist looked very tired. His eyes were red. His hair was standing on end. His hands were shaking as he held open the door. He looked as if he were mad at Ron. Yet, somehow, he seemed very happy, too.

"What are you doing here already?" Dr. Valdez asked.

Ron didn't know what to say. "What a strange way to start a job!" he thought. "First this guy asks me to work for him. Then he asks me what I'm doing here!" He felt like walking away. But that time machine! He had to see if that time machine worked.

Dr. Valdez stepped closer to him. "What happened to you?" he asked. "You're all wet!"

"It's raining out," Ron told him.

"It is?" Dr. Valdez turned to look at the clock on the wall. "9:15! Is it really that late? I've been working all night. I'm nearly ready for the first test. Come in! I just have a few more things to do. While I'm working, I can tell you what I want you to do in the test." He led Ron into the room.

The machines all looked the same as they had the day before. Dr. Valdez went to the control deck and turned a switch. The humming sound got louder again. Dr. Valdez set a dial. He looked at it carefully. Then he set it back the way it was and went on to the next dial.

"The machine is all set to go," he told Ron. "I'm just testing. I've tested every part of the machine. Just a few more dials to go. I want to make sure that nothing can go wrong."

"Sounds like a good idea," Ron said. He looked at the old scientist. Did Dr. Valdez know what he was doing? He was old—and he had been up all night. It would be easy for him to do something wrong. And that would mean Ron's life—or worse.

"Now, here's what we're going to do," Dr. Valdez was saying. "I'm going to send you back 100,000,000 years into the past."

Ron's mouth dropped open. "100,000,000 years!"

he said. "You don't fool around! What do you want me to bring back? A pet dinosaur?"

"No, no. I'll show you in a minute. Now, when we're ready to start, you'll get in the booth, and then I'll send it down on the runners."

Ron went over to the booth and looked down along the runners. The hole under the booth was very deep. "How far down are you going to put it?" he asked.

"All the way down to the bottom," Dr. Valdez said. "100,000,000 years ago, the ground level was much lower than it is now. All of the country was low ground. The middle of the country was all under water. There were a lot of swamps. Then the tall mountains were pushed up. Most of the swamps dried up. That's why I picked this part of the country for my lab. No mountains now. Not too much water then."

"Not too much water?" Ron asked. "I won't end up in a swamp? How can you be sure?"

"Well, I can't be *sure*," Dr. Valdez said. "So I made the booth so that it will keep out water. And I put in a small window. You can look out the window to check on what's out there before you open the door. If the booth is under water, or if you see any other danger, just stay in the booth till I bring it back."

"How long will that be?" Ron asked.

"Well, you'll need some time. You may have to walk quite a way. And you want to be sure to be back in the booth when it comes back."

Ron looked at the booth. He thought about what would happen if it came back without him. He didn't want to be the first cave man!

"So I've set the machine for ten hours," Dr. Valdez went on. "There. That's the last test. Now let's have a cup of coffee."

Dr. Valdez put a pot of water on a hot plate. They sat down at a little table to wait for it to get hot. Dr. Valdez got out some pictures. "Now, here's what I want you to bring back," he told Ron.

Ron looked at the pictures. "Leaves? That's all? You just want me to bring you some leaves?"

"Yes. These are plants that aren't around any more."

"They look like ferns to me," Ron said.

"They *are* ferns," Dr. Valdez said. "Ferns as big as trees."

"Oh," Ron said. He looked at the pictures again.

"You can cut down some leaves with this knife," Dr. Valdez said. He gave Ron a knife with a very long blade. "Do you think you can handle it?"

"Of course," Ron said. "I've used one of these before. In the jungle."

"Good," Dr. Valdez said. He got up to make the coffee. "Then you should be all right. How do you take your coffee?"

"Black," Ron said.

Dr. Valdez gave him a cup. "You'll have ten hours to get the leaves and get back to the booth. Then you'll be back here."

"Right," Ron said. He took a drink of his coffee.

"I don't need to tell you that you'll be alone out there. There will be nothing I can do to help you."

"Don't worry about me," Ron said. "Just run the machine."

"Just remember—ten hours! Ten hours!" the scientist said again. "You've *got* to be in that booth when it come back. If you aren't, I couldn't find you again."

Ron set down his cup. He stood up. "Dr. Valdez, do you think I can't handle the job?" he asked quietly.

"No, of course not! I mean, yes, of course you can! I mean . . . ."

"Is the machine ready?" Ron asked. "Then let's get going."

Dr. Valdez jumped up. He ran over to the control deck and set the machine to full power. The humming sound got louder and louder.

Ron walked over to the door of the lab. He took one last look outside, at the rain falling on the rocky ground all around the lab. Then, holding the knife, he walked over to the booth. He looked at the clock on the wall. It was 10:04. He checked his watch. "Ten hours!" he called out to Dr. Valdez. He opened the door to the booth. "If anything goes wrong," he said, "that $20,000 goes to my mother." He stepped into the booth and pulled the door shut. He locked it carefully on the inside. He could feel the booth moving down the runners. Then he waited.

Nothing happened.

"How will I know when he's going to pull that switch?" Ron asked himself. "Well, I'll just have to wait till he makes his move."

Nothing happened.

He looked at his watch. It was 10:09. "It didn't take that machine this long to warm up before," Ron thought. "I guess the machine didn't work. Rats! I was hoping I'd get to look around in the past. Well, I'll give him two more minutes."

Then Ron looked out the window.

The lab was gone.

The sun was shining.

As far as he could see, the land was flat. Tall grass waved softly in the wind. About a mile away, there was a huge swamp.

And in the swamp, there were two dinosaurs.

Ron felt the hair stand up on the back of his neck. The things were huge!

One was slowly climbing out of the swamp. Its head came up out of the water like a tree. Then its back started to show above the water. More and more of the back—it was as big as a house! Bigger! Then the long tail. It just kept coming out of the water. The end of the tail was hidden in the long grass. But Ron guessed that the dinosaur was eighty feet long.

Ron watched the dinosaur carefully .Would it see the booth? What would he do if it came at him? That thing could knock down the booth with one step. There was no other place to hide.

Nearly ten hours to go before he could get out of there.

But the dinosaur turned and slid back into the water. It went through the water like a huge boat. Its head went down and came back up, dragging long bits of water plants.

Ron looked out the window to see as much as he could see. Where were these fern trees that he had to find?

He couldn't see much through the little window. He would have to get out of the booth.

He unlocked the door and tried to push it open. It wouldn't move.

Now what? The door had been closed from the inside. He had closed it himself. What could be holding it? Had Dr. Valdez pulled something?

He started to feel hot. The sun was beating down on the booth. Then he thought of something. Dr. Valdez had said that the booth would keep out water. Would it keep out air? How soon would he run out of air?

He *had* to get that door open. But what was holding it shut?

He looked out at the ground. Then he looked at the floor of the booth. Yes, it was just as he thought. The floor of the booth was just a little bit lower than the ground.

"Dr. Valdez must have set the booth at the wrong

level," Ron said to himself. "But he made a pretty good guess. He was only a little bit off."

What should he do next? It was only a little bit off, but it would hold the door shut.

He looked at the big knife Dr. Valdez had given him. It was meant for cutting leaves. Was it strong? Could he use it for anything else? He would have to try.

He stuck the end of the knife into the crack of the door. He pushed. The knife held, but the door didn't move.

He pushed harder. He felt something! The door moved! Or did it? Did he only *think* it had moved?

He pushed again. Yes, the door was moving. Slowly, slowly, the door bent out. Crack! The door broke open.

Ron made the hole bigger with the knife. Then he climbed out into the past.

The air felt hot and damp, like the jungle. The tall grass waved around him. It went on and on, as far as he could see. He turned to look at the swamp. Now he could hear the two dinosaurs. They were splashing in the water. They even *sounded* huge.

He looked all around him. Where were the fern trees? Dr. Valdez wanted those big leaves for proof. They would show that he had really been to the past. But where were they? All he could see was grass. He would have to get up on something.

He jumped up and grabbed the top of the booth. He pulled himself up onto it. Now he could see a lot more. The dinosaurs in the swamp. The grass. Another swamp. And yes, some trees. But they were so far away!

Ron checked his watch. It was 11:17. He had lost more than an hour getting out of the booth. Could he get to the trees and back before the ten hours were up?

He started walking. He looked back to make sure that he could see the booth. He didn't want to get lost out here!

He walked and walked. His bad leg was starting to hurt. But the trees didn't seem to be getting any closer. It was so hard to tell just how far away they were. Everything here was so big.

He looked back at the booth again. It seemed very small and far away. He looked back along his path. The grass was still bent down where he had walked. Would it stay bent down? It had better! That might be the only way he could find his way back to the booth.

He walked on.

At last he came to the trees. The huge ferns waved high over his head. It was going to be a real job to climb up there. And it wasn't going to do his bad leg any good.

He sat down to rest for a moment. It was quiet, and warm. The sun felt good. It was funny to think about the rainy day he had left.

He looked up at the trees above him. "OK, trees, here I come!" He got up and put the knife between his teeth. He grabbed the tree as far up as he could. Then he started pulling himself up, inch by inch. The trunk of the tree was smooth. His hands and feet slipped a little as he climbed. But at last he reached the ferns.

He put his arm around one of the ferns and turned to look back the way he had come. He spotted the booth. Then he checked for dinosaurs. The only ones he could see were in the swamp, far away. They didn't seem to care about him at all.

He held onto the bottom of the lowest fern with one hand and took the knife in the other hand. He startd to swing the knife. He hacked at the bottom of the fern next to him. He cut through it, and it fell down into the grass.

One more fern should do it. He put the knife between his teeth again and grabbed the stump of the fern which he had cut. He started hacking at another fern.

He was getting tired. It was hard to hang on to the stump and swing the knife at the same time. He worked faster and faster, making every swing count.

He was working so hard that he didn't look around. He didn't see the huge shadow coming over the grass. He didn't hear the flap of the huge wings. He didn't see the huge claws reaching out for him as they came closer and closer.

Suddenly he was grabbed and lifted high in the air! Huge wings flapped above him. A bird-dinosaur was holding him by one leg. Long claws pushed against his skin.

Ron swung the knife, but he couldn't reach the huge body above him. He grabbed at the claws with his free hand. They only held his leg harder.

The wind rushed past him at each flap of the huge wings. Where was the bird-dinosaur going? Would it eat him now—or later? He swung the knife again at the long, thin legs. But he couldn't lift himself high enough to hit them. He swung and swung the knife. The bird-dinosaur dropped lower, near the ground, but it didn't let him go.

Then he thought of something. The wings! He

threw himself out and back, and swung the knife just as the huge wing came down. The knife ripped into the wing. With a great cry, the bird-dinosaur dropped him.

Ron fell, dropping into the long grass. The knife fell near him. He grabbed it quickly and turned, ready to fight the bird-dinosaur again. But it flapped slowly away.

Ron stood still in the long grass, trying to catch his breath. His arms were so tired that they were shaking. His leg hurt where the claws had held it. But he was all right. He wasn't being eaten.

He checked his watch. It was almost 3:00. He had five hours to get back to the booth. He'd better get started. He didn't have the ferns. He felt bad about it, but there was nothing he could do.

He stood up and looked out over the top of the tall grass. He looked all around him.

Where was the booth?

He couldn't see it over the tall grass.

He could see the fern trees. But they were very far away. That meant the bird-dinosaur had carried him a long way. And he didn't know which way the booth was from the trees.

He was lost in the past.

Comprehension Questions/*Chapter 3*

Directions. Answer these questions about the chapter you have just read. Put an *x* in the box beside the best answer to each question.

1. (C) What did Dr. Valdez do before Ron got to the lab on the morning of the test?

   - ☐ a. He got the pictures of the ferns.
   - ☐ b. He got the time machine ready for the test.
   - ☐ c. He put a pot of water on the hot plate.
   - ☐ d. He sent the booth down on the runners.

2. (B) How far into the past did Ron go?

   - ☐ a. 100 years
   - ☐ b. 1000 years
   - ☐ c. 100,000 years
   - ☐ d. 100,000,000 years

3. (A) When Dr. Valdez told him how far he would go into the past, Ron's <u>mouth dropped open</u>. This means that he was

   - ☐ a. surprised.
   - ☐ b. happy.
   - ☐ c. sad.
   - ☐ d. mad.

4. (D) Dr. Valdez could use the leaves for proof that the time machine worked because

- ☐ a. no one would know what they were.
- ☐ b. no one would know how he got them.
- ☐ c. scientists would know that the fern trees grew only in the past.
- ☐ d. scientists would know that the fern trees grew only around the lab.

5. (D) Ron said that he didn't want to be the first cave man. What did he mean?

- ☐ a. He didn't want to travel to the past.
- ☐ b. He didn't want to get stuck in the past.
- ☐ c. He didn't want to meet any people from the past.
- ☐ d. He didn't want to have a pet dinosaur.

6. (E) What would happen if Ron wasn't in the booth at the end of the ten hours?

- ☐ a. Dr. Valdez would have to wait for him.
- ☐ b. Dr. Valdez would have to send the booth back for him.
- ☐ c. The booth would come back without him.
- ☐ d. A dinosaur would find him.

7. (A) Ron asked, "Dr. Valdez, do you think I can't <u>handle the job</u>?" What does this mean?

- ☐ a. Pick something up
- ☐ b. Work with his hands
- ☐ c. Hold the knife
- ☐ d. Do the job well

8. (C) What was the last thing Ron saw when he was in the booth?

- ☐ a. There was a huge swamp about a mile away from the booth.
- ☐ b. The door of the booth was stuck.
- ☐ c. There was tall grass around the booth.
- ☐ d. The floor of the booth was lower than the ground level.

9. (B) How did Ron get away from the bird-dinosaur?

- ☐ a. He lay down in the tall grass.
- ☐ b. He climbed up in the fern tree.
- ☐ c. He cut its leg with the knife.
- ☐ d. He cut its wing with the knife.

10. (E) How did Ron get lost in the past?

- ☐ a. The booth landed in the wrong place.
- ☐ b. The swamp dinosaurs hurt Ron.
- ☐ c. A bird-dinosaur carried Ron away.
- ☐ d. The fern leaves made Ron sick.

Skills Used to Answer Questions

A. Recognizing Words in Context
B. Recalling Facts
C. Keeping Events in Order
D. Making Inferences
E. Understanding Main Ideas

Comparing Two Things

You know that describing words can tell about people, places or things. Describing words can also be used to compare people, places or things. Look at the underlined words in the sentences below. The underlined words all compare one person or thing with someone or something else.

Each day was colder than the day before.

Main Street is longer than Elm Street.

A rock is harder than wood.

Jean was always smarter than Roy.

The first example compares how cold it was on two days. The second example compares how long two streets are. The third example compares how hard two objects are. The fourth example compares how smart two people are.

The underlined words are comparing words. They show how two people, two places, or two things compare with each other.

Exercise 1

Read the following sentences carefully. Underline the comparing word in each sentence. The first sentence has been done for you.

1. An airplane is faster than a train.
2. Winter days are shorter than summer days.

3. Your grass always looks greener than my grass.

4. The salesman said, "This bed is softer than a cloud."

5. Eddy was much taller than John.

6. One bundle is lighter than the other.

-er *Endings*

You can make a describing word like "cold" into a comparing word, "colder," by adding *-er* to the end of the word. If the describing word already ends in *-e*, you just add *-r* to the end. Look at the examples below.

-er endings			*-r* endings		
old	+ *er* →	older	cute	+ *r* →	cuter
slow	+ *er* →	slower	true	+ *r* →	truer
smooth	+ *er* →	smoother	brave	+ *r* →	braver

Exercise 2

Make the following describing words into comparing words by adding *-er*. If the word already ends in *-e*, just add *-r* to the end. Print your answer on the line beside each describing word. Look at the examples before you start.

Examples: late + *r* → later
strong + *er* → stronger

1. quiet ______________________

2. nice ______________________

3. wise ______________________

4. short ______________________

5. clean ______________________

6. small ______________________

7. wide ______________________

8. white ______________________

9. sweet ______________________

10. tight ______________________

-y *Endings*

If the describing word ends in a *-y*, you must change the ending before you can make it a comparing word. Look at the examples below.

pretty   pretty̸ → prett + *i*+*er* → prettier

happy   happy̸ → happ+*i*+*er* → happier

You must change the *-y* at the end to an *-i*. Then you can add the *-er*.

Exercise 3

Make the describing words below into comparing words by changing the final *y* to an *i* and adding *-er*. Print your answer on the line beside each describing word. Look at the examples before you start.

Example: angry angrier

1. lucky ______________________
2. tricky ______________________
3. noisy ______________________
4. dirty ______________________
5. crazy ______________________

Rules for Making Comparing Words

The boxes that follow give the rules you have learned for making comparing words.

> *Rule 1*
>
> When the describing word ends in a consonant, add *-er* to the end to make it a comparing word:
>
> quick + *er* ⟶ quicker   tall + *er* ⟶ taller

Rule 2

When the describing word already ends in *-e*, just add *-r* to the end to make it a comparing word:

nice + *r* ⟶ nicer wise + *r* ⟶ wiser

Rule 3

When the describing word ends in *-y*, change the *-y* to an *-i* and then add *-er* to the end:

nast~~y~~ + *i* + *er* ⟶ nastier sill~~y~~ + *i* + *er* ⟶ sillier

Exercise 4

Look at the pairs of sentences below. In the first sentence of each pair, the describing word is underlined. Make that describing word into a comparing word by using the rules listed above. Then print that comparing word on the line in the second sentence. The first two pairs have been done for you.

1. She was young.

   She was ____younger____ than her sister.

2. He thought movies were funny.

   He thought movies were ____funnier____ than books.

3. The branch was high.

   The branch was ________ than he could reach.

4. The stars were <u>bright</u>.

   The North Star was ______________________
   than the other stars.

5. The green car was <u>fast</u>.

   The green car was ______________________
   than the blue car.

6. The first test was <u>easy</u>.

   The first test was ______________________
   than the second test.

7. Honey is <u>sweet</u>.

   Honey is ______________________
   than sugar.

8. His clothes felt <u>loose</u>.

   His clothes felt ______________________
   than they did before his diet.

9. That small cat is <u>cute</u>.

   That small cat is ______________________
   than the big cat.

10. He hoped that the tunnel was not <u>narrow</u>.

    He hoped that the tunnel was not ____________
    than the train.

The Newspaper Index

You know how a newspaper is divided into sections. Each section has a different kind of story. That makes it easier to find the stories you want to read. A news story will be in the News section, a sports story will be in the Sports section, and so on. But how can you find each section?

You can find each section by looking in the newspaper's *index*. You will find the index on page 1 or page 2 of the paper. The index is an alphabetical list of what is in the paper. It lists all the sections and tells the pages they begin on. The index also lists things like the Crossword that are only on one page.

Look at the index below. You can see that it gives the pages for all the information it lists.

Index

Amusements	15	Living	11
Classified	19	Local News	4
Comics	26	Sports	29
Crossword	25	Television	14
Deaths	5	US and World News	1
Editorials	9	Weather	2

If you wanted to find the Sports section in this newspaper, you would read down the index until you came to "Sports." Then you would follow the dotted line to the right, to the number 29. This tells you that the Sports section starts on page 29.

Use the index to answer the questions below. Write the page numbers on the lines after the questions.

1. What page is the weather on? *Page:* ____________

2. What page are the editorials on? *Page:* ________

Indexes in Long Newspapers

A long newspaper with many pages and sections is divided into separate smaller parts to make the paper easier to handle. Each smaller part is named with a letter. The first part will be *A*, the second part will be *B*, the third part will be *C*, and so on.

The index below shows what the index in a longer newspaper looks like.

Index

Amusements	C-2	Living	E-1
Classified	C-10	Local News	A-8
Comics	D-7	Sports	F-1
Crosswords	D-6	Television	C-2
Deaths	B-2	US and World News	A-1
Editorials	B-4	Weather	A-2

You can see that each page number has a letter in front of it. The letter tells you which separate part of the paper each page is in. Newspapers that have been divided into separate parts will have letters in front of all the pages. The letters help you find the topics and sections you want to read.

If you wanted to find the Local News in the index above, you would read down the list of topics until you came to "Local News." When you looked to the right for the page number, you would see that Local News starts on page A-8. That means you should turn to the part of the paper marked *A*. Then you would look for the page numbered *A-8*.

Use the index to answer the questions below. Write the numbers on the lines after the questions.

3. What page does the Living section start on?

   *Page E-*________________________

4. This index uses letters *A, B, C, D, E,* and *F*. How many parts are in the newspaper if each letter names a separate part?

   ____

Using a Newspaper Index

You know that long newspapers with many different sections are divided into separate parts. The pages in each part have a letter that helps you find the part. For example, the first part is part A. Each page in part A has the letter *A* in front of the page number. The first page of part A is numbered *A-1* and so on.

Exercise

The index below is from a long newspaper. You can see the letters in front of the pages. Use the index to answer the following questions. Write your answers on the lines after the questions.

Index

1. This index uses the letters *A, B,* and *C.* How many parts are in this newspaper?

____

2. The answers to the following questions are pages listed in the index. The first page number has been filled in to show you how to print your answers.

   Where would you look to find out about:

   a. A fire across the street? B-1

   b. Your favorite comics? ______

   c. The high school football team? ______

   d. The time the movie downtown starts? ______

   e. How to start your own business? ______

   f. A neighbor who died? ______

   g. How the U.S. Senate voted on the tax bill? ______

   h. The editor's opinion of the governor? ______

   i. How much it costs to buy a house uptown? ______

   j. The pastor of the nearest church? ______

4

Lost in the Past

Preview Words/*Chapter 4*

Study the words in the box. Then read the sentences below with your teacher. Look carefully at the words with lines under them.

awake	crawled	killer	steeper
bleeding	gasps	lose	tearing
break	growl	mighty	third
covered	heard	scales	tightly
crashing	heave	slamming	waked

1. <u>Third</u>, he didn't have much time left.
2. The huge feet made a great <u>slamming</u> sound.
3. Ron could hear another sound, a kind of <u>growl</u>.
4. There was a biting, <u>tearing</u> sound.
5. Now Ron <u>heard</u> a scream.
6. Ron could hear the <u>killer</u> dinosaur growling.
7. The dinosaur's skin was <u>covered</u> with scales.
8. It was much <u>steeper</u> here.
9. He stuck his knife in between the <u>scales</u>.
10. He <u>crawled</u> up, pulling himself along.
11. He was holding <u>tightly</u> to the horn over its eyes.
12. It was <u>bleeding</u> from the cuts and bites on its back.
13. It was <u>awake</u> now.
14. With a <u>mighty</u> heave, Ron threw his legs over.
15. <u>Crashing</u> around, he might not see the booth.
16. He had seen it before the dinosaur had <u>waked</u> up.
17. Suddenly the dinosaur gave a mighty <u>heave</u>.
18. His breath came in short <u>gasps</u>.
19. He couldn't <u>break</u> it off.
20. He wasn't going to <u>lose</u> the booth again.

Ron sat down in the tall grass. He had to think.

First, he was lost. He didn't know how far the bird-dinosaur had carried him. And he didn't know which way they had come. So he didn't know where the booth was, or how far away it was.

Second, he was tired. His leg hurt. And he needed something to eat.

Third, he didn't have much time left. In five hours, the booth would go back to 1981. Without him.

He looked at the sun. It was getting low. When would it set? He didn't know what time of year it was now. He should have asked Dr. Valdez. He shouldn't have been in such a hurry to get going. He would have to check everything out more carefully next time.

If there was a next time.

This wasn't getting him anywhere. He had to stop thinking like this. How was he going to find that booth?

What if he went around the fern trees in a big circle? Maybe he could find the path he had made through the tall grass. He might as well try.

He got up. His leg was starting to get stiff. He started to walk through the tall grass. It felt good to be moving again. He didn't have much of a chance of finding the booth. But walking was better than sitting there waiting.

He walked for an hour. He didn't find his path. He couldn't see the booth. He had only four hours left. But he didn't let himself think about it. He just kept walking.

Suddenly he felt the ground shaking. It was shaking harder and harder. Now he could hear something. It was coming closer! Ron stood still, holding the knife tightly, waiting.

Then he saw it.

The head was huge, high above the grass. It was looking around, turning on the big neck. The mouth opened, as big as a cave. And the teeth! Each one was longer and sharper than Ron's knife.

The dinosaur stood and looked around. Ron stood still. Would it see him? If it did—what would it do?

Ron looked down at his knife. It seemed very small. Even a gun wouldn't help him now.

Suddenly the dinosaur started to move again. It was coming at him! Ron dove out of its path. There was a great slamming sound as the huge feet ran past.

Now Ron could hear another sound. It was a kind of growl—but it was louder than any growl Ron had ever heard before. Then there was a biting, tearing sound—and all the time that huge growl went on and on. Ron felt the hair on the back of his neck stand up on end. He wanted to run, to get away from there. He stood up, but the ground was shaking so much that he fell flat again.

Now Ron heard a scream. At the same time, something fell with a great thud. The ground rocked. Then all was quiet.

Ron lay still. One dinosaur must have killed another. Now it would eat its kill. Ron was safe for the moment.

Ron could hear the killer dinosaur tearing at its kill, growling. But soon the ground shook again under its huge feet. The footsteps got quieter and quieter.

The killer dinosaur had run away.

Ron jumped up. He wanted to go and look at the dead dinosaur. "Why not?" he thought. "This may be how I will get my food for the rest of my life!"

He could see the wide path where the killer dinosaur had run through the tall grass. And there, not far away, was the dead dinosaur.

It was lying on its side. There were big marks on it, left by the other dinosaur's teeth and claws. All around it, the grass was down flat from the fight.

Ron walked up to it. Even lying on its side, not moving, the thing was huge. Its side rose high over his head, like a small hill.

A hill! That was just what he needed! Quickly, he climbed onto the dinosaur's tail. He walked carefully along it. The dinosaur's skin was covered with scales. He almost slipped on them, but he kept on his feet.

Ron climbed onto the body. It was much steeper here. His feet kept slipping out from under him. At last he crawled up, on his knees. He pulled himself up by sticking the knife in between the scales. It was slow work—but he was getting higher.

Now he was above the tall grass. He hung onto the knife and looked carefully around.

The grass went on and on, as far as he could see. Here and there, a few fern trees stuck up through it. Far away, a bird-dinosaur was flying. But there was no booth.

It had to be out there somewhere! Ron looked and looked. But he just couldn't see it.

Wait! What was that? So far away—so small. Ron had to look right into the sun. He tried to shade his eyes. Yes! It was the booth!

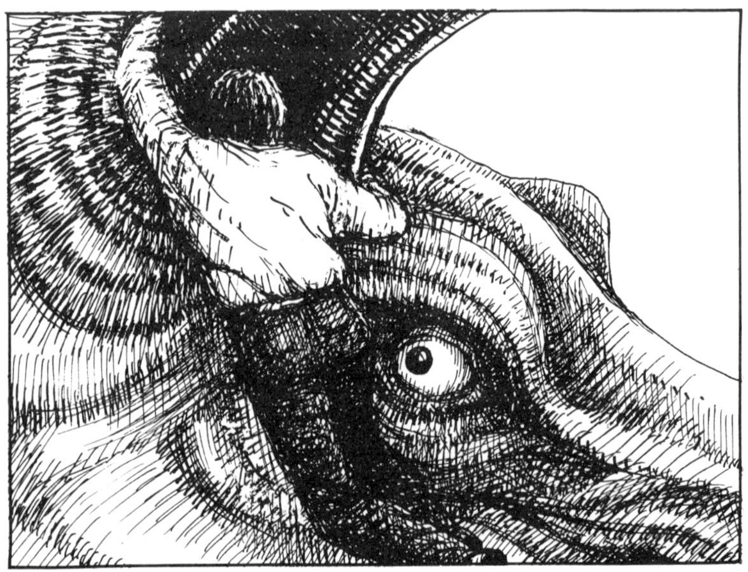

Ron checked his watch. It was 5:02. He had three hours left. Could he get there in time? Would he get there before the sun set?

Suddenly Ron began to fall. The ground was shaking under him. No—not the ground! It was the dinosaur! The dinosaur was waking up! Ron was sliding down the dinosaur's side. He grabbed for the scales on the dinosaur's skin. But nothing stopped him.

The dinosaur was trying to stand up. Ron was thrown up and down. Now the dinosaur lifted its head. Ron could see the huge mouth. And the teeth! He tried to stick the knife into the dinosaur's skin. But nothing worked.

The dinosaur got its back legs up, then its front legs. Ron was thrown down along the neck. Suddenly the head came up. Ron was falling. He dropped the knife and reached out. He grabbed something.

Now the dinosaur was standing up. Ron found that he was holding tightly to the horn over its eyes. His legs hung down on one side—very close to the teeth. He tried to bring his legs up, but they kept slipping down again.

The dinosaur was badly hurt. It was bleeding from the cuts and bites on its back. But it was awake now. And it was ready to fight.

Ron could see one of its eyes. The eye kept turning. The dinosaur was trying to look at him. It was trying to see what was hanging onto its head. Then it started to shake its head. Ron held onto the horn for dear life.

The dinosaur shook its head harder. Then it tried to scrape Ron's legs against its side. With a mighty heave, Ron threw his legs over to the other side of its head. Now the dinosaur turned the other way. It began to run in a circle, trying to scrape Ron off.

Ron pulled and kicked and grabbed and pulled some more. Now he was sitting across the dinosaur's head, with one leg hanging down on each side. His feet were just in front of the dinosaur's eyes. He still kept his arms tightly around the dinosaur's horn.

Now what was he going to do?

The dinosaur was running in big circles. It kept shaking its head. Then it threw its head hard over to one side. Ron started to slide off. He kicked on the other side, trying to hold himself on.

The dinosaur threw its head over the other way. It turned to run that way, too.

Was it turning because Ron had kicked it? Ron tried kicking it on the other side, right in front of its eye. Yes, the dinosaur turned again. It turned to the side Ron kicked it on. He could steer the dinosaur!

He felt a new hope running through him. Could he do it? Could he? It was crazy! But it was his only chance!

Hanging onto the horn, he looked all around. Where was the booth now? How would he see it, crashing around like this?

The sun! The sun had been over the booth! He had seen it before the dinosaur had waked up. That was only a few minutes ago. He could find it that way!

Quickly, he looked at the sun. It was low in the sky, off to his right. He kicked the dinosaur with his right foot. The dinosaur turned and ran to the right.

Now it was turning too far to the right. Ron kicked it with his left foot. It turned back. It was running fast—right into the sun!

Ron looked and looked for the booth. He had to keep kicking the dinosaur, first on one side and then on the other. The sun was getting lower and lower. It was hard to see. Was he right? Was this the way to the booth? Or was he going the wrong way—fast?

Or had he gone right by the booth? The sun was in his eyes. The dinosaur kept shaking its head and throwing him around. Maybe he had gone right by the booth—and hadn't seen it.

Suddenly the dinosaur gave a mighty heave. Ron was thrown off. He flew through the air, head first.

For a moment, he saw something shine in the tall grass. Then—bang! He hit the ground, rolling over and over in the tall grass.

He got to his feet fast. Where was that dinosaur? He could feel the ground shaking under its feet. But it couldn't find him. For the first time, he was glad that the grass was so tall. Soon, the dinosaur went away.

Now he could think. He had seen something as he fell. Something shining. What was it? *Where* was it?

He started to walk. Where was it? Where? Could he find it? Soon he was running.

He ran through the tall grass. His hands pushed the grass out of his way. His breath came in short gasps. His feet ran and ran.

And suddenly, there it was. In front of him. Just as he had left it.

The booth.

He threw himself down on the ground beside it. He had found it! He was safe! He could go home! He would go home and never, never come back.

He looked at his watch. It was 5:52. He still had more than two hours to go. He sat by the booth, looking down at the ground.

He waited.

Soon he looked up. He looked around. Then he looked at his watch. It was 6:04. Just two hours to go.

He was safe. But he hadn't done his job. He didn't have anything to take to Dr. Valdez for proof.

He sat by the booth for a few more minutes. Then he slowly got up. He had to find *something* for Dr. Valdez. The old man was going to want something to show for his $20,000.

He walked around the booth. He looked all around on the ground. Nothing.

What about some of the grass? He pulled at it. It wouldn't come up. He couldn't even break it off. If only he still had his knife!

He stood quietly. He could hear the dinosaurs moving around in the swamp. Maybe he could find something there. Maybe he could catch a fish or something.

He started to walk to the swamp. He walked for a few minutes. Then he stopped. He turned around and looked at the booth. It was already almost hidden in the tall grass.

No way. He wasn't going to lose that booth again.

He started to walk back to the booth. Then he looked down at the ground.

There it was. Just what he needed.

A dinosaur egg—a new one!

Dr. Valdez would have his proof. Everyone would believe a baby dinosaur.

Ron stuck the egg under his arm like a football. He walked quietly back to the booth. He climbed into the booth through the hole he had made. He sat down on the floor to rest. And wait. And hope that he never saw another dinosaur as long as he lived.

The sun set. It was very dark in the booth. He waited.

At last it was 8:04. At that moment, he felt the booth moving up, up. He stood up. Now he could see the lights of the lab. As soon as the booth stopped moving, he opened the door.

Dr. Valdez was running to him. "What happened to the booth?" he called. "The door is a mess! What was it like in the past? What did you see? What did you find? Did you get the leaves?"

"Hey! One question at a time!" Ron snapped. Didn't Dr. Valdez care what had happened to *him*? "No, I didn't get your leaves."

"You didn't? Why not? What happened? What. . . ."

"Don't worry. I'll tell you all about it," Ron said, as he climbed out of the booth. He thought for a moment. It would be quite a story to tell. Fighting the bird-dinosaur. Being lost in the past. Riding a dinosaur! He shook his head. "It was quite a trip," was all he said.

"Quite a trip?" Dr. Valdez was nearly crying. "But the proof! You didn't bring back anything for proof!"

"I didn't say that. Here, take this." He gave Dr. Valdez the dinosaur egg.

He looked at the old scientist. Suddenly, Ron couldn't help smiling. "You're going to be a father," he said.

Comprehension Questions*/Chapter 4*

Directions. Answer these questions about the chapter you have just read. Put an *x* in the box beside the best answer to each question.

1. (E) What was the main thing Ron had to do in this part of the story?

   ☐ a. Kill a dinosaur
   ☐ b. Get away from the bird-dinosaur
   ☐ c. Find the booth
   ☐ d. Find the fern trees

2. (D) Ron felt the hair on the back of his neck stand up. What made this happen?

   ☐ a. The wind was blowing through his hair.
   ☐ b. The bird-dinosaur was pulling on his hair.
   ☐ c. He was very scared.
   ☐ d. He was very angry.

3. (A) The dinosaur was going to eat its kill. What does this mean?

   ☐ a. Kill something to eat
   ☐ b. Eat what it had killed
   ☐ c. Get into a fight
   ☐ d. Get killed and eaten

4. (B) Ron climbed up on the dinosaur

- ☐ a. to see what it looked like.
- ☐ b. to get a closer look at its scales.
- ☐ c. to look for the booth.
- ☐ d. to look for his knife.

5. (C) What happened just before the dinosaur woke up?

- ☐ a. Ron saw the booth.
- ☐ b. One dinosaur killed another.
- ☐ c. Ron lost his knife.
- ☐ d. Two dinosaurs came out of the swamp.

6. (C) What happened when Ron kicked the dinosaur with his right foot?

- ☐ a. The dinosaur howled with pain.
- ☐ b. The dinosaur stood still.
- ☐ c. The dinosaur ran to the left.
- ☐ d. The dinosaur ran to the right.

7. (B) How did Ron get off the dinosaur?

- ☐ a. He climbed down over the tail.
- ☐ b. The dinosaur threw him off.
- ☐ c. He fell into the dinosaur's mouth.
- ☐ d. He climbed onto the top of the booth.

8. (D) Why was Ron glad that he could bring back the dinosaur egg?

- ☐ a. He wanted to do the job he had set out to do.
- ☐ b. He knew that Dr. Valdez wouldn't let him come back without it.
- ☐ c. He wouldn't get any money if he didn't bring it back.
- ☐ d. He wanted to see a baby dinosaur.

9. (A) "Hey! One question at a time!" Ron <u>snapped</u>. What does this mean? Ron talked

- ☐ a. in a sad way.
- ☐ b. in a happy way.
- ☐ c. in a crazy way.
- ☐ d. in an angry way.

10. (E) How did Ron think Dr. Valdez would use the dinosaur egg?

- ☐ a. To raise a baby dinosaur
- ☐ b. To prove that the booth had been in the past
- ☐ c. To study the egg in the lab
- ☐ d. To give Ron a present for making the trip to the past

Skills Used to Answer Questions

A. Recognizing Words in Context — B. Recalling Facts
C. Keeping Events in Order — D. Making Inferences
E. Understanding Main Ideas

Comparing Two Things or Actions with "More"

Comparing Two People, Places or Things

You know that one way of making a describing word into a comparing word is by adding *-er* to the end of the word. Below is a review of the three rules for making describing words into comparing words:

Rule 1: When the describing word ends in a consonant, add *-er* to the end to make it a comparing word:

quick + *er* ⟶ quicker

Rule 2: When the describing word already ends in *-e*, just add *-r* to the end to make it a comparing word:

nice + *er* ⟶ nicer

Rule 3: When the describing word ends in a *-y*, change the *-y* to an *-i*, and then add *-er* to the end:

nasty̸ + i + *er* ⟶ nastier

Now look at this new rule.

Rule 4

When the describing word has three or more syllables, leave the describing word as it is and put the word "more" in front of it:

beautiful: 3 syllables ⟶ more beautiful
amazing: 3 syllables ⟶ more amazing

Exercise 1

Make the describing words below into comparing words. First count the syllables in the describing word. Write this number in the row marked "Number of Syllables." Then print "more" and the describing word. The first one has been done for you.

	Describing Words	Number of Syllables	Comparing Words
1.	valuable	4	more valuable
2.	mysterious	________	________
3.	intelligent	________	________
4.	disgusting	________	________
5.	expensive	________	________

Exercise 2

Make the describing words on the next page into comparing words. Count the syllables to help you decide which rule to use. Add an *-er* ending if the word has only one or two syllables. Use the word "more" in front of the describing word if it has three or more syllables. Print your answer on the line beside each word. Look at the examples before you start.

Examples:

interesting	4 syllables	more interesting
quick	1 syllable	quicker

Describing Word	Comparing Words
1. serious	______________________
2. wonderful	______________________
3. bright	______________________
4. wild	______________________
5. frightened	______________________
6. unusual	______________________
7. hard	______________________
8. terrible	______________________
9. mean	______________________
10. cool	______________________

Comparing Two Actions

You know that some describing words tell about actions. They describe how something was done. You remember that words that describe actions usually end in *-ly*. Here are some examples of words that describe actions:

noisily   angrily   softly   swiftly

If you want to compare two actions, put "more" in front of the word that describes an action:

noisily ⟶ more noisily
angrily ⟶ more angrily
softly ⟶ more softly
swiftly ⟶ more swiftly

Exercise 3

Look at the pairs of sentences below. In the first sentence of each pair, the word that describes an action is underlined. Make the describing word into a word that compares two actions by putting "more" in front of it. Then print the comparing words on the line in the second sentence. The first two have been done for you.

1. He can swim quickly.

   He can swim more quickly than his father.

2. Mary drives carefully.

   Mary drives more carefully than anyone in her family.

3. George does his work happily.

   George does his work ____________ than Jack does.

4. My cat walks quietly.

   No animal can walk ____________ than my cat.

5. I can fix that flat tire easily.

   I can fix that flat tire ______________________ than you can.

6. She skates smoothly across the ice.

   She skates ______________________________ across the ice than her brother does.

7. Bill read aloud clearly.

   Bill read aloud ____________________________ than Allan.

8. The woman ran bravely into the fire.

   The woman ran ____________________________ into the fire than the fireman did.

9. Pat worked steadily all day.

   Pat worked ______________________________ all day than Liz did.

10. He answered the judge's questions honestly.

    He answered the judge's questions ____________ than the robber did.

News Stories

Reading the headlines in a newspaper is a quick way to find out what happened one day. The headlines also help you to pick out the stories you want to read. Look at the sample news story on the next page. The headline says "Civil Rights Leader Shot." If you are interested in this story, you will want to know more than the headline tells. You can learn more by reading more of the story.

Where the Story Comes From

Sometimes the first word in a story after the headline will be the name of a place. It will be printed in big letters. It might say NEW YORK. It might say WASHINGTON. It might say PARIS. This tells you what city the story comes from. If no place is named, the story comes from the same place as the newspaper.

When the Story Happened

Sometimes you will see a date at the beginning of the story. Sometimes there is a date after the name of the place the story came from. The date tells you when the story happened. If no date is given, it means that the story happened on the same day that the newspaper was printed.

Look at the news story on the next page. Print the answers to the following questions on the lines after the questions. Use capital letters where the newspaper does.

Civil Rights Leader Shot

FORT WAYNE, May 29—Vernon Jordan has been shot. He is the director of the National Urban League. And he is one of the nation's top black civil rights leaders. Jordan was critically wounded when he was shot. It happened in a motel parking lot early today. The police said they had no suspects.

Jordan, 44, was shot twice in the stomach. He had surgery at Parkview Memorial Hospital. The hospital said his condition was "stable but serious."

The FBI in Washington has been in touch with the Fort Wayne police. The FBI has no information about the motive for the shooting.

1. Where does this story come from?

____

2. When did the story happen?

____

The First Paragraph

You know that news stories tell the facts about something that happened. You can usually find out the most important facts by reading the first paragraph of a story. The first paragraph will tell you what happened. The first paragraph will tell you who did it or who it happened to. The first paragraph will also tell you when and where the story happened.

Look at the first paragraph of the sample news story about the civil rights leader. The first paragraph says:

> Vernon Jordan has been shot. He is the director of the National Urban League. And he is one of the nation's top black civil rights leaders. Jordan was critically wounded when he was shot. It happened in a motel parking lot early today. The police said they had no suspects.

The underlined parts of the first paragraph tell:

Who: Vernon Jordan

What: was shot

Where: in a motel parking lot

When: early today

This first paragraph tells you all the most important facts. The first paragraph answers the questions: Who? What? When? Where?

Reading a News Story

This page gives the beginning of a news story. Read it carefully, and then answer the questions below. What you have learned about headlines and news stories will help you.

Montreal Hospital Fire

MONTREAL, December 8—More than half of the Montreal fire department fought a large fire today. The blaze was at a major downtown hospital. More than 600 patients had to be carried out of the hospital. No injuries were reported.

Notre Dame hospital is one of the largest in Quebec Province. The police reported that the firefighters got control of the blaze quickly.

The fire was reported at 6:36 A.M. It started in the garbage in the kitchen, which is in the basement. Flames quickly moved up the walls to the floors above.

Exercise 1

Answer the questions below, using the story you have just read. Print your answers on the lines below the questions. Use capital letters where the newspaper does.

1. What does the headline say the story is about? Print the one most important word in the headline.

   ____

2. Where does this story come from?

   ____

You have learned that the first paragraph of a news story answers these four questions:

Who? What? When? Where?

Here are the first two sentences of the news story you have just read. You can see that four groups of words have been underlined. Each word group is marked with a capital letter. Read the sentences and look at the underlined word groups.

More than half of the Montreal fire department (A) fought a large fire (B) today (C). The blaze was at a major downtown hospital (D).

Exercise 2

Each group of words that is underlined in the sentences above answers one of the four questions: Who? What? When? or Where? Use the letter of each word group to tell which question the word group answers.

Print the question in the space after each letter. The first question has been printed to show you how to do the others.

1. What question is answered by word group A?

   Who?

   ____

2. What question is answered by word group B?

   ____

3. What question is answered by word group C?

   ____

4. What question is answered by word group D?

   ____

5

2481

Preview Words/*Chapter 5*

Study the words in the box. Then read the sentences below with your teacher. Look carefully at the words with lines under them.

August	computer	proudly	thousands
building	factories	smoothly	unloaded
camera	flashlight	surprised	world
cellar	lucky	swimming	zipped
clicking	offices	themselves	zoomed

1. You might find out that they moved the world.
2. I could take a camera with me and take pictures.
3. He would get to the future on August 12, 2481.
4. At last he found his flashlight.
5. They were putting up a building.
6. He was in the cellar hole.
7. They were running themselves.
8. You're lucky they could see this box!
9. The car made a small clicking sound.
10. Jit saw that Ron looked surprised.
11. The food is unloaded here and sent all over the city.
12. He watched another car sail by smoothly.
13. We have schools, labs, doctors, swimming pools.
14. The buildings have offices in them.
15. "836,482 people live there," Jit said proudly.
16. As they zoomed at the huge wall, Ron got scared.
17. The car turned and zipped to the building.
18. They moved along, looking at stores and factories.
19. They saw thousands of people.
20. The building machines ran on computer tapes.

Ron had gone back 100,000,000 years into the past. He had come back safely.

The time machine had worked.

And at first Ron didn't care if he ever saw it again.

That trip to the past had been too much.

It wasn't the dinosaurs that had worried him. He could fight those.

It was the grass. The tall grass that went on and on and on. That was full of hidden dangers. That almost kept him from finding the booth. It was the grass that had bothered him. And he didn't want to go near the machine that had put him there. He would not test the machine again.

But after a few days, Ron began to think about it again. At last he said to himself, "I've got to sit down and think this thing through."

He sat down in his living room and put his feet up. He leaned back and closed his eyes. He let his thoughts go.

After all, he thought, the future wouldn't be like the past. There would be people there. No dinosaurs. And no grass. What could go wrong?

The more he thought about it, the better it looked. No one had ever been to the future. No one knew what it would look like. He would be the only one who knew. Wouldn't that be great?

Then he thought of one more thing. He had already told Dr. Valdez that he would do the job. They had even signed a paper. He couldn't turn it down now! What if the word got out? People would think that he was scared! He might lose other jobs.

Yes, he would have to make another trip with the time machine. But he was going to help a lot more with the plans!

He got up and put on his coat. Soon he was in his Jeep and on his way to the lab.

Dr. Valdez was walking up and down in the lab. "I can't send you too far into the future," he was saying. "We don't know what's there. We can study the past. But we can't study the future. So I don't want to send you too far. I want to be sure that you will land safely. I don't want you to get there and find out that they moved the world!"

Ron walked over to the case at the side of the room. He looked at the dinosaur egg he had found in the past. It was keeping warm under a light. Then he looked at the other things in the case.

"Hey, what about this, Doc?" he called. "You've already sent the booth to 2481. It came back OK, with this newspaper in it. So you know it's safe. Send it to 2481 again."

Dr. Valdez stopped walking. He turned to look at Ron. "What a good idea! Why didn't I think of that?"

"I've been doing a lot of thinking about this next trip," Ron said. "I have some other ideas, too."

"What?"

"Fix a trap door on the booth. So I can get out if something is in front of the door."

"Yes, yes," Dr. Valdez said. He looked at the door of the booth, where Ron had made a big hole with the knife. The hole was still there. "Yes. I'll cut a trap door in the top. What else do you want?"

"Let me stay a longer time. Then I won't have to hurry. I don't know what it'll be like till I get there. You know, like those fern trees you wanted. I didn't know how far away they would be till I got there. If I'd had more time, I wouldn't have had to worry so much about finding the booth. I could have got back to the trees." He looked down at his dinosaur egg. He gave the egg a little pat. "I like this better anyway," he said.

"Yes, yes. More time," Dr. Valdez said. "You can have more time. I just have to set the dial." He ran his hands through his long hair. "You can have all the time you want. Why not? You could be gone for years. But you would still come back the same moment you left."

"Good. Let's say three days. That should give me all the time I need. So I'll need to take some food and clean clothes with me, too. I can take my pack in the booth. Now, what will you want me to bring back from the future?" Ron asked.

"I don't know. I've thought and thought about it. But I just don't know what you'll find."

"Well, I'll just look around. Hey, I know! Pictures! I could take a camera with me and take some pictures."

"That's a good idea," Dr. Valdez said. "But bring something else back, too. People can say that pictures are a fake."

"All right," Ron said. "I'll see what I can find."

The next morning they were ready for the trip to the future. The new trap door had been cut in the top of the booth. Ron had packed the booth with everything he needed.

Ron watched Dr. Valdez set the dials on the control deck. He would get to the future at 1:00 in the morning on August 12, 2481. And he could stay until August 15, 2481.

He checked the things in the booth one more time. Then he shook hands with Dr. Valdez. "See you in three days," he said.

"See you in a few minutes," Dr. Valdez said.

Ron got into the booth. The sound of the machine got louder and louder. Through the window of the booth, Ron could see the red light come on. Any moment now, he would be in the future. He could see Dr. Valdez put his hand up to the switch. Suddenly it was dark.

And he was falling!

The booth was falling, falling .... He didn't know which end was up.

Crash! The booth hit something and crashed onto its side. Ron was thrown down in a heap of food and clothes.

He lay still for a long time.

At last he started to move. Did he have any broken bones? He tried his arms, then his legs. No, no broken bones. The heap of clothes had broken his fall.

Now what? How was he going to get out? The booth was lying on its door. The trap door! It was sure a good thing that Dr. Valdez had put it in.

Ron dug through the clothes and food in the dark. At last he found his flashlight. He turned it on and shined it on the end of the booth. Oh, no! Where was the trap door? Then he saw that he was looking at the floor.

He turned around. He was lucky that the booth wasn't any smaller. Then he shined the light at the other end of the booth. Yes, there was the trap door, right in front of him. He opened it and crawled out.

Now, where was he?

He shined the light all around him. The ground was flat and smooth. Far away above him, he could see city lights. They were all around him, but not near him. Where was he? Why weren't there any lights here?

He had wanted to come at night. That way, maybe no one would see him. But now . . . . He didn't know what to do. He would have to wait till it got light.

He crawled back into the booth. He packed his food and clothes back into his pack. Then he got out of the booth and sat down to wait.

Soon it wasn't as dark as it had been. Ron looked up. He could see the sky now. He seemed to be at the bottom of a huge, deep hole.

It got lighter and lighter. Now he could make out some machines by the top of the hole.

The machines were huge. They weren't like anything he had ever seen before. Yet he was sure he knew what they were for. They were for putting up a building.

And he was in the cellar hole.

"I get it!" Ron said to himself. "Dr. Valdez and I thought we were so smart. We thought it would be safe if I came in the same *year* as before. I should have come on the same *day*. I'll bet it doesn't take very long to dig a cellar hole these days."

He put on his pack. He walked and walked. At last he came to the side of the hole. It was so big! He looked

up at the big machines. They were huge!

How big were the people who ran them?

It was getting later. The sun must be coming up. The sounds of the city started to get louder.

The machines started to move.

They came slowly down, right down the sides of the hole. Each one was bigger than Dr. Valdez's lab. Ron looked for the people who were running them.

No one was running them. They were running themselves.

They came at Ron. He ran. They kept coming. Ron ran for the booth. He didn't know what good it would do. These machines could run right over it.

They were getting nearer and nearer. He had to go *somewhere.* He got to the booth and jumped up on it.

The machines stopped.

A moment later, a little car flew down to the bottom of the hole. Ron watched it come. Now what?

The car landed on the ground next to the booth. A man jumped out. Ron was glad to see that the man wasn't any bigger than he was.

"What are you doing down here?" the man asked. "You could have been killed! These machines just smooth out the ground. They don't see very well. They aren't meant to. They won't bump into each other. But they couldn't see you! You're lucky they could see this box!" he shouted, pointing at the booth. "Now, what are you doing down here? How did you get this box down here?"

What should Ron tell him? What *could* he tell him? Should he tell the man what had really happened? Why not? He might even believe him!

"Do you know anything about time machines?" Ron asked the man.

"Time machines?" the man asked. "You mean, do I know how they work? No way! I don't even really know how *this* works," he said, patting his flying car.

"But you believe in time machines?" Ron asked.

"*Believe* in them? Why not?"

"How long have they been around? Who invented them?" Ron asked.

The man shook his head. "I don't know who invented them. They've been around for years and years. For as long as anyone can remember. But why are you asking me all these questions?"

"Well," Ron said, "this booth is part of the very first time machine."

"It is? Wow!" the man said. He looked at the booth. "It doesn't look like much, does it?"

"Well, most of the machine is back at the lab," Ron said.

"So you're from the past! That's why you look so funny! Those clothes you have on! And that's why you sound so funny when you talk! When are you from?"

"1981."

"500 years ago," the man said. "How about that! Well, what do you think of 2481?"

"I haven't seen much of it yet," Ron said.

"Oh, no, I guess you haven't," the man said. "Hop in my car. I'll give you a ride and show you the city."

"That would be great!" Ron said. "By the way, my name is Ron Wells."

"I'm glad to meet you, Ronwells. My name is Jit."

"No, not Ronwells. Ron Wells. Wells is my last name," Ron said.

"Your last name?" Jit asked. "I don't know what you mean."

"Don't you have two names?" Ron asked.

"No," Jit said. "You have two names? Ronwells and Wells? I don't. . . ."

"Never mind," Ron said. "Just call me Ron."

"You have *three* names?" Jit asked.

"Can we see the city now?" Ron asked.

He got out his camera as they went over to the little car. The car was waiting, floating just above the ground. They got in. The seats were deep and soft. Ron looked at the dash. It was full of dials and switches and buttons. There was no steering wheel.

Jit turned a switch, pushed a few buttons, and sat back. The car rose right up in the air. When it got up out of the big hole, it made a small clicking sound. Then it took off over the city on a long, smooth line.

Jit saw that Ron looked surprised. "We're locked onto the city car beam," he told Ron. "500 years ago, did you still have *roads*? Boy, I'll bet there were a lot of car crashes in those days."

"Yes, there are—were," Ron said. He watched another car sail smoothly by, then another and another. "This does seem to be a lot safer."

"I should think so! To think of *people* driving cars!" Jit said. "Now, over there is City Hall."

Ron looked where Jit was pointing. He gasped. City Hall was nearly as big as the city he had left! It went for block after block. "It must be a mile high!" Ron shouted.

"Nearly a mile," Jit said. "Now we're coming to the Foods Building. This is where food from other parts of the country comes in. It is unloaded here and

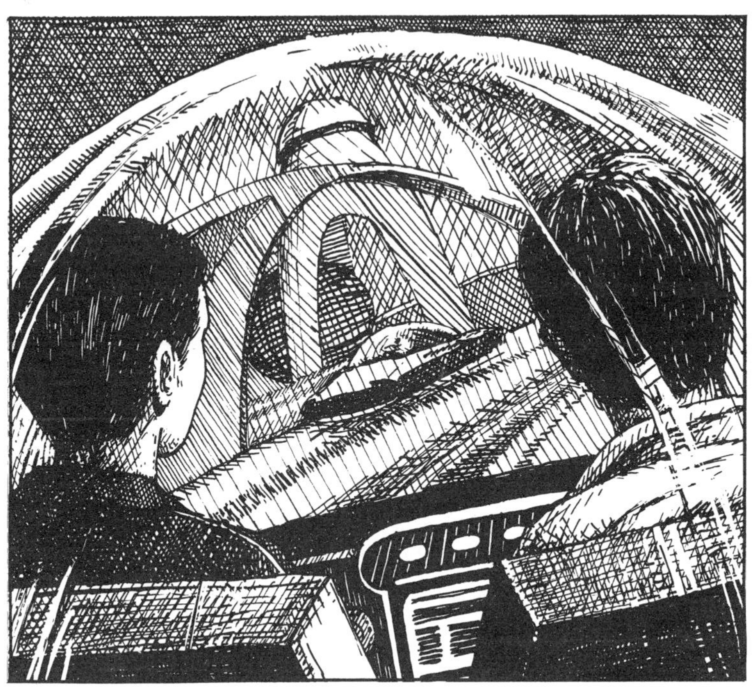

sent to the stores all over the city. Now, over here . . . ."

"Wait a minute!" Ron said. "Stores! Roads! *People*! Where are they? I thought this was a city! But all I can see are trees and grass! It looks like a park down there. And then, every few miles, one of these huge buildings. Where are the stores? Where are the houses? Where are the people?"

"In the buildings! That's my building over there. 836,482 people live there," Jit said proudly. "Stores? We have 50,000 of them."

"What about schools? What about? . . ."

"We have schools, labs, doctors, swimming pools. You name it, we've got it."

"But where do people work?" Ron asked.

"Most people work right in the building they live in. The buildings have offices and factories, too. But some people work outside, like me. A lot of people feel sorry for me, but I *like* working outside. Where do you work?" he asked Ron.

"Oh, I go on a lot of jobs. Most of them are outside."

Jit smiled. "Then you know what I mean. But wait a minute. You're from before the big buildings. In 1981 everything was in lots and lots of *little* buildings, wasn't it? Little buildings all over the place. And roads. No green places in the cities at all!"

"Well, we do have parks," Ron said. "I mean, we *did* have them. But nothing like this."

"But what did you do when you wanted to get out? What if you wanted to go camping or fishing or something like that?" Jit asked.

"Oh, there were places you could go. But it might take a few hours to get there," Ron said.

Jit looked at him sadly. "That's too bad," he said. "Oh, well. I'll show you the inside of my building."

He pushed another button on the dash of the car. The car turned and zipped to the building that Jit had pointed to. As they zoomed at the huge wall, Ron got scared. Would the car turn? He looked at Jit. Jit didn't look scared at all. The car didn't slow down. The huge wall came nearer. Then, at the last moment, a door in the wall opened and the car zipped in.

The car ran along a hall till it came to a big room. The room was full of cars, line after line, piled high. Their car stopped, let them out, and parked itself neatly.

Jit led Ron through a door and into the main part of the building. There were long streets with stores along them. Ron saw a school yard full of children.

The streets were full of people. The people were moving quickly, but they were standing still. Then Ron saw that the streets were moving!

Jit showed Ron how to hop onto the moving street. They moved quickly along, looking at the stores, factories, and houses. They saw thousands of people. And all this was on just one level. There were many, many levels above and below them! Ron took pictures of everything.

"This is quite a place," Ron told Jit. "I never thought that the future would be like this. It's—well, it's kind of nice!"

Jit smiled. "I'm glad you like it," he said. "But I've got to get back to work now. The building machines run on computer tapes. They can work for five hours by themselves. But their computers will be running out of tape soon. I have to get back and check their work. Then I can put in some new tapes."

"Sounds like a good job!" Ron said. "OK, let's go."

They went back to the parking room. Jit's car met them by the door. They got in, and the car pointed itself at the wall and zoomed off. The wall opened up, and they zipped through.

Ron looked back at the huge building they had come from. It was hard to picture all the levels it had in it. All those people, and houses, and stores. All in one building! He had seen it—but he wasn't sure he believed it!

The car took them quickly back to the cellar hole. They got out, and the car set itself down on the ground and shut itself off.

Jit went right to work. He called in the machines and started to take out their computer tapes.

Ron walked along the cellar hole. The machines had done a lot of work while they had been gone. The building would go up fast.

Ron stood looking down into the cellar hole. He thought about the huge building that would be there, and all the people that would live there.

Then he looked again.

The booth wasn't there.

Directions. Answer these questions about the chapter you have just read. Put an *x* in the box beside the best answer to each question.

1. (A) Ron thought he couldn't turn the job down. He asked, "What if the word got out?" What was he afraid of?

   ☐ a. People might hear about it.
   ☐ b. The dinosaur might get away.
   ☐ c. Ron might tell Dr. Valdez's secret.
   ☐ d. Dr. Valdez would not give his word.

2. (B) How did Ron know it would be safe to travel to 2481?

   ☐ a. A scientist had studied it.
   ☐ b. Dr. Valdez told him.
   ☐ c. The booth had been there before.
   ☐ d. The monkey had been there before.

3. (E) Why did the booth fall when it got to 2481?

   ☐ a. A building machine bumped into it.
   ☐ b. Dr. Valdez had put it up on the runners.
   ☐ c. Dr. Valdez hadn't known about the cellar hole.
   ☐ d. The ground level of all the country had changed.

4. (C) What happened just before Ron found the trap door of the booth?

- ☐ a. He tried to open the door.
- ☐ b. He shined his flashlight on the wrong end of the booth.
- ☐ c. He shined his flashlight all around the cellar hole.
- ☐ d. He put his clothes into his pack.

5. (D) Jit didn't know who had invented the time machine. What did this tell Ron?

- ☐ a. Ron and Dr. Valdez did not really make history.
- ☐ b. Ron would never get back to 1981.
- ☐ c. Dr. Valdez had not really invented the time machine.
- ☐ d. Jit didn't know anything about 1981.

6. (B) How did Jit run the flying car?

- ☐ a. By pushing buttons on the dash
- ☐ b. By turning the steering wheel
- ☐ c. By putting in a computer tape
- ☐ d. By talking to it

7. (D) Why did Jit feel a little bit sorry for Ron?

- ☐ a. He thought that Ron didn't have a job.
- ☐ b. He thought that life in 2481 was much better than life in 1981.
- ☐ c. He thought that no one would want to come to 2481.
- ☐ d. He thought that Ron was lost.

8. (C) When Jit showed Ron around the big building, where did they go first?

- ☐ a. The moving sidewalk
- ☐ b. The factories
- ☐ c. The stores
- ☐ d. The school yard

9. (A) Ron looked at the huge building. It was hard to picture all the levels it had in it. What does this mean?

- ☐ a. He could take a picture with his camera.
- ☐ b. He couldn't see the levels from the outside.
- ☐ c. It was hard for him to think about it.
- ☐ d. No one had ever seen it before.

10. (E) What was the main thing Ron had to worry about at the end of this part of the story?

- ☐ a. He couldn't find anything for proof.
- ☐ b. He had lost the booth again.
- ☐ c. He had no place to stay.
- ☐ d. He couldn't steer a flying car.

Skills Used to Answer Questions

A. Recognizing Words in Context | B. Recalling Facts
C. Keeping Events in Order | D. Making Inferences
E. Understanding Main Ideas

Comparing Three Things

You know that you can compare two people, places or things by adding *-er* to the end of a describing word:

February is a <u>short</u> month.
February is a <u>shorter</u> month than June.

You can also compare three or more people, places or things by adding *-est* to the end of a describing word. Look at the underlined words in the sentences below. The underlined words all compare three or more people, places or things:

February is the <u>shortest</u> of the months in the year.

They climbed the <u>highest</u> mountain in the world.

Her lawn was the <u>greenest</u> one on the whole street.

The first example compares February with the other eleven months of the year. The second example compares one mountain with all the other mountains in the world. The third example compares one lawn with all the other lawns on the street. The underlined words show how three or more people, places or things compare.

Exercise 1

Read the sentences on the facing page. Underline the word in each sentence that compares three or more people, places or things. Remember that words that compare three or more people, places or things end in *-est*. The first sentence has been done for you.

1. She bought the newest car in the show room.
2. They found a stream in the thickest part of the forest.
3. Ted walked to the nearest gas station when his car broke down.
4. Sue was the youngest person ever to graduate from that school.
5. He thought his father was the strongest man in the world.
6. The children stared at the lion because he was the wildest animal they had ever seen.

Adding -est

You can add *-est* to the end of a describing word if you want to compare three or more people, places or things. The rules for adding *-est* to the end of a word are the same as the rules for adding *-er* to the end of a word. The rules are given below.

Rule 1

When the describing word ends in a consonant, add *-est* to the end to compare three or more people, places or things:

quick + *est* → quickest
low + *est* → lowest
tall + *est* → tallest
long + *est* → longest

Rule 2

When the describing word already ends in *-e*, just add *-st* to the end to compare three or more people, places or things:

brave	+ *st*	⟶	bravest
wide	+ *st*	⟶	widest
nice	+ *st*	⟶	nicest

Rule 3

When the describing word ends in *-y*, change the *y* to an *i*, and then add *-est*:

lazy	+	laz~~y~~	+	*i*	+	*est*	⟶	laziest
funny	+	funn~~y~~	+	*i*	+	*est*	⟶	funniest
tricky	+	trick~~y~~	+	*i*	+	*est*	⟶	trickiest

Exercise 2

Each describing word below ends in a consonant. Make these describing words into words that compare three or more people, places or things by adding *-est* to the end of each word. Print your answers on the lines beside the describing words.

Read Rule 1 again before you start. It will help you know how to answer the questions.

1. poor ____________________

2. dark ____________________

3. bold ____________________

4. sharp ______________________

5. fair ______________________

Exercise 3

Each describing word below ends in an *-e*. Make these describing words into words that compare three or more people, places or things by adding *-st* to the *-e* at the end of each word. Print your answers on the lines beside the describing words.

Read Rule 2 again before you start. It will help you know how to answer the questions.

1. ripe ______________________

2. fine ______________________

3. dense ______________________

4. simple ______________________

5. blue ______________________

Exercise 4

Each describing word below ends in *-y*. Make these describing words into words that compare three or more people, places or things by changing the final *-y* to an *-i*, and then adding *-est* to the end of each word. Print your answers on the lines beside the describing words.

Read Rule 3 again before you start. It will help you know how to answer the questions.

1. tasty ____________________

2. fluffy ____________________

3. shiny ____________________

4. shady ____________________

5. chilly ____________________

Exercise 5

On the next two pages there are ten groups of three sentences. The underlined word in the first sentence of each group is a describing word. You can see that the first describing word is <u>sunny</u>.

The underlined word in the second sentence of each group is the describing word made into a word that compares two people, places or things. You can see that the first comparing word is <u>sunnier</u>.

Your job will be to make each describing word into a word that compares three or more people, places or things. You can see that the word *sunniest* has been printed on the line in the third sentence. *Sunniest* compares three rooms that are sunny.

The second group of three sentences also has been done for you. Read the sentences and look at the words that have been underlined or printed.

Then read the other groups of sentences. Print the words that compare three people, places or things on the lines in the sentences. To make each comparing word, use one of the three rules for adding *-est* to the end of a word.

1. This front room is sunny.
   This front room is sunnier than that back room.
   This front room is the
   sunniest ______________________
   one in the house.

2. Taking a bus is cheap.
   Taking a bus is cheaper than renting a car.
   Taking a bus is the
   cheapest ______________________
   way to travel.

3. Jeff was neat.
   Jeff was neater than his brother.
   Jeff was the
   ____
   person in the family.

4. These pink flowers are bright.
   These pink flowers are brighter than those white ones.
   These pink flowers are the
   ____
   flowers I've ever seen.

5. The doctor was rich.
   The doctor was richer than the fire chief.
   The doctor was the
   ____
   woman in town.

6. It is safe to fly in an airplane.
It is safer to fly in an airplane than to ride in a car.
The

___

way to travel is to fly in an airplane.

7. The baby in the yellow blanket is tiny.
The baby in the yellow blanket is tinier than the baby in the white blanket.
The baby in the yellow blanket is the

___

baby in the hospital.

8. The tiger cub was tame.
The tiger cub was tamer than the full-grown lion.
The tiger cub was the

___

animal in the circus.

9. The old rope was weak.
The old rope was weaker than the new rope.
The old rope was the

___

one he owned.

10. The dirt road was bumpy.
The dirt road was bumpier than the cement road.
The dirt road was the

___

road in the state.

The Classified Section

Every newspaper has a section called "Classified." This is the section with columns of advertisements or ads. The section is called "Classified" because the ads are arranged by *classes*. This means that the ads are arranged by the *kinds* of things they tell about. The headings in the Classified section tell you what the ads are about.

Having the same kind of ads in the same part of the Classified section makes it easier to find the ads you want to read. If you were looking for a job, for example, you would look under the headings "Help Wanted" or "Employment." If you wanted to find a new place to live you would look under the heading "Apartment" or the heading "Houses For Sale." And if you wanted to find the car ads, the headings "Cars" or "Automobiles" would tell you what ads to read.

When you want to buy something, look first for the name of whatever you want to buy. If you don't see that name, look for the heading "For Sale." Ads that don't have their own headings usually are listed together under "For Sale."

Classified ads are quite small. They have to say a lot in a small space. Almost every word in an ad tells you a new fact about what is being sold or rented. You should read an ad slowly. You will see a period or a comma after every few words. Stop reading at every punctuation mark. Ask yourself what fact the words before each mark tell you.

Besides using few words, there is a second way to keep an ad short. The writer of the ad makes the words themselves shorter. In many ads some of the words have letters missing. You can tell what the whole words are by knowing the kinds of words the ad would use.

There are some words that usually are given with letters missing. You will see these short forms of words in many ads. For example, look at the last words of the car ad below. The short form "aft." is used instead of the whole word "after." The ad tells you to call about the car after 7 P.M.

Car Ads

Read this ad for a used car very carefully. You can see how much information it gives in a few words.

1979 PLYMOUTH FURY. 44,000 mi. Runs well. Radio, tinted glass. $1100. 662-9003, aft. 7 P.M.

You can see that this ad begins by telling you the model of the car and the year it was made. It also tells you how many miles the car has been driven.

Print your answers to these questions. Use the same punctuation the ad does.

1. What year was this car made? ________________

2. a. How many miles has this car gone? ________

b. What short form of the word "miles" does this ad

use? ________________________________

This car has gone a lot of miles. But the owner says the car is in good shape. That is what the words "Runs well" mean. Still, you should check out the car very carefully for yourself. You should always check out everything in an ad for yourself.

You can see that this car ad tells you two things the car has: a radio and tinted glass windows. The ad also tells you the price: $1,100. And it gives you a telephone number to call after 7 P.M. You can talk to the owner and find out where and when you can look at the car.

Reading a Classified Ad

Remember that an ad tells many facts in very few words. You should stop reading the ad at the punctuation mark after every word or two. Ask yourself what facts those one or two words tell.

An Ad for a Used Car

The ad below is for a used car. Read the ad to find out what facts it tells you.

FORD MUSTANG. 1968. Like new. Many new parts, radio, heater. $700 firm. 782-8076 aft. 6 P.M.

Exercise 1

Use the information in the ad to answer these questions. Print your answers on the lines below the questions. Use capital letters where the ad does.

1. Print the two words that tell you what kind of car is for sale.

   ____

2. What year was this car made?

   ____

3. Print the two words that tell you this car is in good condition.

____

4. How much does this car cost?

____

5. What word tells you that the owner will not accept any less money for the car?

____

An Ad for an Apartment

The ad below is for an apartment. The ad uses many short forms of words. Read the ad and look at the short ways of giving the words. Notice the periods after the short forms.

OAKLAND. Pine St. Sunny 1-bdrm apt. New building. $325. No pets. Tel. 253-0692.

Exercise 2

Use the information in the ad to answer these questions. Print your answers on the lines below the questions. Use capital letters where the ad does. And use periods after the short forms of words.

1. What city is this apartment in? The first word of the ad tells you the name of the city.

____

2. The first short form of a word is for the word "Street."

   a. What is the name of the street the apartment is on?

   ____

   b. Copy the short form of the word "Street."

   ____

3. This apartment has one bedroom. Find this information in the ad. On the lines below print the short ways of giving each of these words.

   a. bedroom

   ____

   b. apartment

   ____

6

The Man from the Future

Preview Words/*Chapter 6*

Study the words in the box. Then read the sentences below with your teacher. Look carefully at the words with lines under them.

beginning	east	north	south
build	famous	once	stomped
changed	happening	own	supper
cheat	joker	rules	unlocking
dragged	leaning	someday	upset

1. It was happening again.
2. The first number shows how far north the place is.
3. It shows how far south it is.
4. The second number shows how far east or west it is.
5. You have to know a lot of rules for time travel.
6. Things from the future could cheat people.
7. Jit was unlocking a door.
8. This is much better than your own time.
9. He stomped away.
10. It was leaning to one side.
11. The machine dragged it away.
12. He was mad at that joker, Jit.
13. They had a big supper.
14. The booth had blurred and changed.
15. He couldn't think why Dr. Valdez looked so upset.
16. He wanted to hear about everything at once.
17. He told him the story from beginning to end.
18. I was kind of hoping I'd be famous.
19. I could build a set of buttons into the control deck.
20. Someday I will make more trips through time.

Ron stood looking into the cellar hole. He couldn't believe his eyes. The booth was gone! It was happening again! Just like his trip to the past! The booth was gone!

Would he be stuck in the future? No! He had to find that booth!

He turned fast and looked for Jit. Jit must know where it had gone.

Jit had got out the plans for the new building. He was looking at them carefully when Ron ran up to him.

"My booth! They took away my booth!" Ron told him.

Jit looked up from his plans. "Of course," he said. "We can't put the building on top of it." He went back to his plans.

"But where is it? I need it!" Ron shouted at him.

"I don't know where it is," Jit said. "The machines must have got rid of it while we were gone." He made some notes on the side of one of the plans.

"But how am I going to get home?" Ron shouted.

Jit rolled up his plans and put them away. "What are you so worried about?" he asked. "Why do you need that old box? You don't have to travel in an *old* time machine. Use one of our *new* ones!"

Ron stopped short. What a great idea! He could come back in a nice new booth. He would come back looking like a man from the future! Wouldn't that old Dr. Valdez be surprised! Ron couldn't wait to see the old guy's face when he stepped out of the new booth.

"Where can I find one of these new time travel machines?" he asked.

"Oh, there's one in every building," Jit said. He started to walk over to one of his big machines. "Just ask at the office."

Ron walked along with him. "Who runs the time machines?" he asked.

"No one. You do it yourself. You put in the numbers for where you want to go. You know the numbers for your lab, don't you?"

"The numbers?"

"*You* know—the numbers for the place you want to go. There are numbers for every place in the world. They're the same ones we use to tell the flying cars where to go." He took a little book out of his pocket and showed it to Ron. "See? This book gives all the numbers for the places you can go in this city. Here's the number for the new building, right here. 1012-8751-301. The first number shows how far north or south the place is. The second number shows how far east or west it is. The third number shows how far up or down it is. See, I had to write in the number for the bottom of the cellar hole."

Ron held the book in his hand. It was made out of a very smooth, thin paper. Just like that bit of newspaper back at the lab!

Back at the lab.... Would he ever see the lab again?

Jit was still talking. "There are buttons on the time travel machine, just like the ones in my flying car. When you want to give your numbers to the machine, you just push the buttons. That's all there is to it."

"But I don't know my numbers," Ron said.

"Oh, you must know your numbers," Jit said. "Even little children know their numbers. So that's all you have to do. Just put in your numbers and your day and time. Then the machine will ask you a few questions. If you pass the test...."

"The test?" Ron asked weakly.

"*You* know—a test to see if your trip should be made. There are a lot of rules you have to know for time travel! We can't have everyone just jumping around through time. They could mess up the past very badly. Or they could use things from the future to cheat people. You have to show that you know the rules. And you have to show that you know how to take care of yourself."

"I see," Ron said sadly. "I used to think that I knew how to take care of myself," he said to himself.

Jit was unlocking a door at the bottom of one of the building machines. He opened the door and looked at the computer tapes that ran the machine. He started to pull the tapes out. "So if you pass the test," he went on, "then you put in your money."

"Money? How much?" Ron asked.

"That goes by how far you're going. It's a lot. It costs a lot of money to run one of those machines, you know. But you have a lot of money, don't you? I mean, you got *this* far."

"Yes, but not on my own money," Ron said. "I was just testing the machine!"

"Oh, I see." Jit shook his head. "Well, you can save up for it," he said. He started putting new tapes into the machine. "You'll want to get a job anyway. You'll have to work while you wait for your turn."

"Wait for my turn?" Ron asked. He was starting to feel sick.

"Yes," Jit said. "I'm afraid so. It'll take nine or ten years. Maybe a little longer. Everyone wants to take a time trip these days. But your turn will come up sooner or later."

"*What!*" Ron shouted. "I have to pass a test. I have to find out those numbers. I have to get up the money. And then I still have to wait!"

"What's the matter with that?" Jit asked. "I thought you liked it here! This is much better than your own time, isn't it?"

"I *like* my own time!" Ron said. "And I can just see it! By the time I get back to 1981, I'll be older than my mother!"

He stomped away. He walked along the side of the huge hole. In back of him, one of the big machines started to move down to the bottom of the hole. It started to do the work that the new computer tape told it to do.

Ron didn't look at the machine. He just walked and walked. But he was still walking next to the big hole. There seemed to be no end to it.

On the other side of him were trees. They seemed nice, kind of like home. After all, his home was only a few miles from here—500 years ago. But now it looked as if he would never see his home again.

He had always lived with danger. He had always taken care of himself.

But now there was nothing he could do.

With his hands in his pockets and his head hung low, Ron walked along the side of the hole.

Suddenly he could hear a humming sound in back

of him. He turned around. Coming at him fast was Jit's flying car.

The car stopped next to him. Jit leaned out, smiling. "They found it!" he called. "The machines found your booth. Hop in."

Ron got in the car. Jit pushed a button, and the car zipped back to the work place.

Ron jumped out of the car before it stopped. There was the booth! And it was a mess!

It was standing up, but it was leaning to one side. It was all banged up. Its door was nearly all the way off. "Wait till Dr. Valdez sees this!" Ron said.

"I'm sorry about that," Jit said. "The machine dragged it away."

"How did you find it?" Ron asked.

"I just had each machine run back its tapes. Every move they make is on those tapes. So I just ran the tape back to this morning. I read what the machines did while we were gone. I'm sorry that I didn't think of it sooner."

"That's OK." Ron was too happy to be mad. "Now all I have to do is set the booth up where it fell."

Where it fell!

Oh, no! When the booth had been in 1981, it had been at the old ground level. Then, when it came to 2481, it was standing on thin air. So it fell—into the new cellar hole.

What if he left the booth at the bottom of the cellar hole? When it went back to 1981, it would be deep under the ground!

"What's wrong?" Jit asked. Ron told him about the ground levels.

"But you've got two more days!" Jit said. "In two

days, the building will be up to the ground level."

"In two days?"

"Sure! And the machines will know just where to put your booth. Don't worry about a thing," Jit said.

"Thanks," Ron said. He looked around. Suddenly, those trees by the hole looked a lot more like the ones at home.

The next day was a lot of fun for Ron. He took the flying bus all over the city. He looked at more of the big buildings. He took more pictures for Dr. Valdez. He walked in the woods with Jit. He watched the new building go up.

The big machines were great. Jit was the only person on the job. Yet the building went up so fast! Things were happening everywhere at the same time. The building was going up before his eyes.

The second day, Ron stayed at the work place. The building had come a long way. But it had a long way to go. Would it be ready in time?

The day went by. Ron got more and more worried. It was getting late. But the building wasn't even near the ground level. What would he do? How would he get the booth up there?

Jit came up and stood next to him. "You look worried," he said. "What's up?"

"It's what isn't up," Ron said. He pointed into the cellar hole. "That's not going to be ready in time."

"Don't worry about a thing! Watch what happens at the end of the day," Jit said. He walked away without saying any more.

It started to get dark. The machines stopped.

The building was still not up to the ground level.

Ron watched Jit closing down the machines. He

felt mad. Mad at that joker, Jit. Mad at old Dr. Valdez. And mad at himself, too. Why did he need those two? Why couldn't he take care of himself any more?

Then Jit walked over to another machine. Ron had never seen it before. It was even bigger than the other building machines. What did it do? Could it help him?

Jit pushed some buttons on the machine. The machine started to roll. It rolled to where the booth was standing. It picked up the booth. Then it rolled over to the hole and went down in. When it got to the bottom, it rolled over to a spot below where Ron was standing. Then it lifted the booth up on a long arm. Up, up the booth came. At last it was at ground level. Ron could step right into it.

Jit came up in back of Ron. "What do you think?" he asked. "Its computer tapes know just where to put the booth. That should take care of you."

"That's great, Jit!" Ron said.

"Let's get something to eat before you go," Jit said. "And I have something to give you."

They got into Jit's flying car and flew to his building. They had a big supper. They told each other about their lives and their jobs. They talked about their city, about how it had changed from 1981 to 2481.

It was getting late. Ron almost didn't want to go. But his three days in the future were almost up. It was time to get back to the booth.

It was nearly 1:00. Jit and Ron were standing by the cellar hole. Jit gave Ron a new book with the numbers of every place in the city. "You can use the book when you want to come back," Jit said. "I put my numbers on the first page." Ron just smiled. How could he tell Jit that he would never come back?

Ron stepped into the booth. He waved at Jit. He shut the door of the booth as best he could. The machine rolled across the new floor of the new building. It stopped just over the place where the booth had hit the cellar floor. It held the booth at ground level.

Inside the booth, Ron sat down to wait. He felt sad that he would never see Jit again. But he was glad that he was going home. And he was glad that he would never have to make another trip through time.

Back at the lab, back in 1981, Dr. Valdez had watched Ron get into the booth. When everything was ready, he had called out, "5 . . . 4 . . . 3 . . . 2 . . . 1 . . . now!" and pulled the switch. He had watched the booth carefully. The booth had blurred.

And changed!

It was a mess! It was leaning to one side. It was all banged up. The door was nearly all the way off. What had happened?

What had happened to Ron?

Dr. Valdez jumped down from the control deck.

"Ron!" he shouted, running to the booth. "Ron! Ron!"

Inside the booth, Ron saw light coming in the window. Then he could hear someone shouting his name. He jumped up and opened the door. As he stepped out of the booth, he saw Dr. Valdez running to him. He couldn't think why Dr. Valdez looked so upset. Then he remembered the booth. To Dr. Valdez, the booth had changed from one moment to the next.

"I'm sorry about the booth," Ron started to say.

But Dr. Valdez grabbed Ron and looked him up and down. "Are you all right? Are you all right?" he asked over and over again.

"I'm OK," Ron said. He smiled. Dr. Valdez seemed to be really worried about *him*, not just the machine. Maybe the old boy wasn't so bad after all. "I'm OK. I'm really OK!"

"You're really all right? You aren't hurt? You're

sure? That booth looks as if it had been hit by a car! Well, come on. Let's have a cup of coffee, and you can tell me all about it."

Ron made the coffee, and they sat down to drink it. But Dr. Valdez couldn't sit still. He jumped up and walked up and down the lab. He asked Ron question after question about the trip to the future. He wanted to hear about everything at once.

At last Ron got him to calm down. He told the old scientist the story from beginning to end. When he was done, they just sat and looked at each other for a moment.

"And you say that they had never heard of me?" Dr. Valdez asked at last.

"No, they hadn't," Ron said. "They didn't know who had made the first time machine."

Dr. Valdez looked down at the floor. "I was .... I was kind of hoping I'd be famous," he said.

"Well, 500 years is a long time," Ron said. "I'm sure you'll be famous now, in 1981. That's what counts. You have your proof now. When will you call in the other scientists? And the newspapers?"

But Dr. Valdez didn't seem to hear him. "That book of numbers .... Now, that's a good idea! I could build a set of buttons into the control deck. Maybe there would be some way that I could build them into the booth, too! Then you wouldn't have to be so afraid of getting lost! And then .... Oh, this is great! There's so much more work to do on this! I'll have to run a lot more tests. Would you ... ?"

Ron stood up. He smiled down at the old man. "Maybe someday," he said. "Maybe someday I will make some more trips through time for you. But not now. Right now, I'm going to go home. And stay there for a while."

He walked out of the lab. There was his good old Jeep. His good old 1981 Jeep. He got into it and drove down the road to the city. The good old 1981 city.

It was good to be home.

Comprehension Questions/*Chapter 6*

Directions. Answer these questions about the chapter you have just read. Put an *x* in the box beside the best answer to each question.

1. (D) Why didn't Jit get upset when they found that the booth was gone?

   ☐ a. He didn't care what happened to Ron.
   ☐ b. He knew just where the booth was.
   ☐ c. He didn't see why Ron needed the booth.
   ☐ d. He thought that Ron had hidden the booth.

2. (B) What was one of the things that Ron would have to do to use a time machine in 2481?

   ☐ a. Ask Dr. Valdez to set it up
   ☐ b. Ask Jit to set it up
   ☐ c. Pass a test
   ☐ d. Change his clothes

3. (B) How long did Jit think Ron would have to wait to use a new time machine?

   ☐ a. Two days
   ☐ b. All fall and winter
   ☐ c. One or two years
   ☐ d. Nine or ten years

4. (E) What was the <u>main</u> idea that Ron got from Jit about the time machines in 2481?

- ☐ a. He didn't know the rules.
- ☐ b. He would never have enough money.
- ☐ c. There weren't very many of them.
- ☐ d. They wouldn't do him much good.

5. (A) Ron <u>stomped</u> away from Jit. What was he doing, and why?

- ☐ a. Walking hard because he was mad
- ☐ b. Running fast because he was scared
- ☐ c. Running fast because he was happy
- ☐ d. Crawling slowly because he was tired

6. (A) Jit was <u>closing down</u> the machines. What does this mean?

- ☐ a. Closing the doors
- ☐ b. Stopping them for the night
- ☐ c. Getting rid of them
- ☐ d. Turning them over

7. (C) What did Jit do just before Ron got into the booth to go back to 1981?

- ☐ a. He closed down the machines.
- ☐ b. He gave Ron a book of time travel numbers.
- ☐ c. He showed Ron around the city.
- ☐ d. He told Ron about the time machines of 2481.

8. (C) What did the biggest machine do after Ron got into the booth?

- ☐ a. It lifted the booth up to the ground level.
- ☐ b. It rolled down into the cellar hole.
- ☐ c. It carried the booth over to a place above where it had fallen.
- ☐ d. It got rid of the booth.

9. (E) Why was Dr. Valdez so upset when Ron came back from the future?

- ☐ a. Ron didn't bring back anything for proof.
- ☐ b. Ron said that he wouldn't make any more trips.
- ☐ c. The booth looked so bad that he thought Ron had been hurt.
- ☐ d. The booth looked so bad that he thought Ron had hurt it.

10. (D) Why did Dr. Valdez want to run more tests at the end of the story?

- ☐ a. He was a scientist, so he wanted to know more about the time machine.
- ☐ b. He was an old man, so he believed that the time machine hadn't worked.
- ☐ c. He knew that Ron wanted to go to the future again.
- ☐ d. He knew that other scientists still wouldn't believe him.

Skills Used to Answer Questions

A. Recognizing Words in Context	B. Recalling Facts
C. Keeping Events in Order	D. Making Inferences
E. Understanding Main Ideas	

Comparing Three Things with "Most"

Comparing Three People, Places or Things

You know that you can make a describing word into a word that compares three or more people, places or things by adding *-est* to the end. A review of the three rules for adding *-est* to the end of a describing word follows.

Rule 1: When the describing word ends in a consonant, add *-est* to the end to compare three or more people, places or things:

quick + *est* ⟶ quickest
low + *est* ⟶ lowest

Rule 2: When the describing word already ends in *-e*, just add *-st* to the end to compare three or more people, places or things:

nice + *st* ⟶ nicest
wise + *st* ⟶ wisest

Rule 3: When the describing word ends in *-y*, change the *-y* to an *-i*, and then add *-est* to the end:

nast~~y~~ + *i* + *er* ⟶ nastier
sill~~y~~ + *i* + *er* ⟶ sillier

Now look at this new rule.

Rule 4

When the describing word has three or more syllables, leave the describing word as it is and put the word "most" in front of it to compare three or more people, places or things:

beautiful: 3 syllables ⟶ most beautiful
amazing: 3 syllables ⟶ most amazing

Exercise 1

Make the describing words below into comparing words. First count the number of syllables in the describing word. Write this number in the row marked "Number of Syllables." Then print "most" and the describing word. The first one has been done for you.

	Describing Word	Number of Syllables	Comparing Words
1.	disgusting	3	most disgusting
2.	talented		
3.	comfortable		
4.	plentiful		
5.	dependable		
6.	colorful		

Exercise 2

Make each describing word below into a word that compares three or more people, places or things. Count the syllables to help you decide whether to use an *-est* ending or "most" in front of the word. Print your answer on the line beside each word. Look at the examples before you start.

Examples:

uncomfortable most uncomfortable

hard hardest

1. clear ____________________

2. reliable ____________________

3. enormous ____________________

4. swift ____________________

5. warm ____________________

6. elegant ____________________

7. kind ____________________

8. inexpensive ____________________

9. depressing ____________________

10. dull ____________________

Comparing Three or More Actions

You remember that words that describe actions usually end in *-ly*. You know that you can compare two actions by putting the word "more" in front of the word that describes the action.

noisily ⟶ more noisily
angrily ⟶ more angrily
swiftly ⟶ more swiftly

If you want to compare three or more actions, you put the word "most" in front of the word that describes the action:

noisily ⟶ most noisily
angrily ⟶ most angrily
swiftly ⟶ most swiftly

Exercise 3

Make each word that describes an action below into a word that describes three or more actions by putting "most" in front of it. Print your answer on the blank line beside each word. Look at the examples above before you start.

1. secretly ____________________
2. gladly ____________________
3. slowly ____________________
4. quietly ____________________
5. loudly ____________________

Exercise 4

Seven groups of three sentences are given below. The underlined word in the first sentence of each group describes an action. You can see that the first underlined word is *gracefully.* The underlined words in the second sentence compare two actions. You can see that the words *more gracefully* are underlined in the second sentence.

Make the word in the first sentence that describes one action into a word that compares three or more actions by putting the word "most" in front of the describing word. Then print "most" and the describing word on the line in the third sentence. The first two sentence groups have been done for you.

1. Joan dances gracefully.
   Joan dances more gracefully than Mary.
   Of the whole class, Joan dances the
   most gracefully ________________ .

2. The judge spoke seriously.
   The judge spoke more seriously than the lawyer did.
   Of all the people in the court, the judge spoke the
   most seriously ________________ .

3. The man in the circus walked steadily across the narrow rope.
   The man walked more steadily across the rope than the bear did.
   Of all the performers in the circus, the man walked
   the ________________________________
   across the rope.

4. The man stepped onto the boat lightly.
The woman stepped onto the boat more lightly than the man.
The child stepped onto the boat the

____

of all the passengers.

5. The mailman looked at the broken lock crossly.
The owner of the house looked at the broken lock more crossly than the mailman did.
The policeman looked at the broken lock the

______________________________ of all.

6. During the play, Mary spoke her lines nervously.
Fred spoke his lines more nervously than Mary did.
Of all the people in the play, Jean spoke her lines the

______________________________ .

7. The secretary greeted the child cheerfully.
The nurse greeted the child more cheerfully than the secretary did.
Of all the people in the office, the doctor greeted the child the

______________________________ .

Television Listings

Every newspaper has television listings. The listings tell you what shows are on television each day. You can find the listings by looking in the newspaper index under "Television" or "TV."

The television listings are arranged by time. For example, the listings given below tell you what shows are on at 8:30 P.M. and what shows are on at 9:00 P.M.

You can see that the listings tell you the channels and the names of the shows. The listings also tell you more about some of the shows. For example, the movie on channel 27 at 8:30 is described.

8:30 P.M.
(2) **News**
(4) (10) **Little House on the Prairie**
(5) **Baseball**
Red Sox and Yankees
(6) (7) **M*A*S*H**
(27) **Movie**
"The President's Lady," with Charlton Heston. This movie reveals the scandal about Andrew Jackson's wife.

9:00 P.M.
(2) **National Geographic**
"Antarctica: Desert of Ice, Sea of Life"
(6) (7) **House Calls**
(38) **Network News**
(25) **Another Voice**

The first thing you look for when you read television listings is the time you want to watch television. Then look down the list of channels. If a show is on more than one channel, you will see more than one number for the show. The channel numbers tell you if a show is on a channel you can get where you live.

The listings also give the name of the show. This helps you choose what to watch. If there is an explanation of the show, that helps you too You can see that the 8:30 movie has an explanation. You are told who is in the movie and what the movie is about.

Look at the listing again. Print the answers to these questions. Use capital letters where the listings do.

1. How many shows are on at 9:00 P.M.?

____

2. Look at the 8:30 shows. Besides M*A*S*H, what other show is on more than one channel?

____

3. What channel is "Another Voice" on?

____

4. On the line below, print the name of the show at 9:00 that is on channels 6 and 7.

____

5. On the line below, print the name of the baseball team that the Yankees are playing at 8:30.

____

Using Television Listings

You know that the newspaper gives television listings. These listings tell you the times, channels, and names of the shows on television each day.

Sample television listings appear below.

6:00 P.M.
(2) Zoom
(4) (5) (6) (7) (10) (12) News
(27) Wild Kingdom
"Elephants"
(25) The French Chef
"Salad"
(56) Star Trek

6:30 P.M.
(2) Sesame Street
(4) (10) News
(5) (12) Candid Camera
(6) (7) 60 Minutes
(27) Bowling
(25) Soundstage

Exercise

Use the television listings to answer the following questions. Print your answers on the lines below the questions. Use capital letters where the listings do.

1. What two times do the television listings show?

   a. ______________________________

   b. ______________________________

2. How many channels have a news show at 6:00 P.M.?

____

3. What animals is the show "Wild Kingdom" about?

____

4. What food is "The French Chef" about?

____

5. What two channels have the show "60 Minutes"?

   a. ____

   b. ____

To the Instructor

Purpose of the Series

Teachers charged with the responsibility of providing instruction for adults and older students with reading difficulties face a major problem: the lack of suitable materials. Stories written at the appropriate level of maturity are too difficult; stories easy enough to read independently are too childish.

The stories in the Adult Learner Series were written to solve the readability problem. The plots and characters in these stories are suitable for adults and older students, yet the stories can be read easily by very low-level readers.

The principal goal of the series is to provide interest and enjoyment for these readers. To this end, every attempt has been made to create a pleasant reading experience and to avoid frustration. The plots move quickly but are kept simple; a few characters are introduced and developed slowly; the same characters are utilized throughout a text; sentence structure and vocabulary are carefully monitored.

A secondary goal is to help adults explore and develop everyday life skills. Lessons and exercises about a variety of life skills provide adults and older students with the basic competencies they need for success in this fast-paced world.

Rounding out the structure of the series are exercises for developing vocabulary skills, comprehension skills, and language skills.

Reading Level

The stories in the Adult Learner Series are all written at second grade reading level. It should be kept in mind, however, that the stories were written for adults: people with a wider range of experience and larger speaking and listening vocabularies than those of elementary school children. Thus, there are some words and some events which might present difficulties for elementary school students but which should not pose problems for older beginning readers.

Besides the slightly increased complexity of vocabulary and plot, the writing style itself has been adapted for older beginning readers. Every effort was made to make the prose sound natural while maintaining simplicity of structure and vocabulary. The repetition of words and phrases has been carefully controlled to permit maximum learning of new words without producing a childish effect.

The reading level of the stories was established by the use of the *Fry Readability Formula.* According to this formula, the range of reading levels of the chapters of this book is from grade 1.3 to 2.4.

Ninety-four percent of the words used in *Doctor Valdez* are included in *3,000 Instant Words* by Elizabeth Sakiey and Edward Fry; 89 percent are among the first 2,000 words in that book, which lists the 3,000 most common words in the English language, ranked in order of frequency. The first 100 words on the list and their common variants [*-s*, *-ing*, etc.] make up 50 percent of all written material. The first 300 words and their variants make up 65 percent of all written material. Because readers encounter a relatively small number of words so frequently, they must be able to recognize the Instant Words immediately to be effective readers.

The story line of *Dr. Valdez* presents some concepts—geological, social, and language change (all predictions of the future)—which may be new to some students. For them, and perhaps for all students, a discussion of these concepts might improve comprehension and enhance the element of reading for pleasure which is the primary purpose of all the stories in the Adult Learner Series.

Structure and Use of the Text

Each book in the Adult Learner Series is divided into several units. Each unit follows a regular format consisting of these sections:

Preview Words

Twenty words from each chapter are presented for students to preview before reading. Those words that were expected to give students the most difficulty were chosen for previewing. The preview section includes all words of more than one syllable that are not among the first 2,000 words on Sakiey and Fry's list of 3,000 Instant Words. The words are listed first in alphabetical order and then shown again in story sequence in sentences based on the chapter.

The twenty sentences match the chapter in readability; students can read the sentences independently. With some classes the instructor may want to read the words and sentences aloud for students to repeat and learn. In very structured classes, the words could also be used for spelling and writing practice.

Story

The primary purpose of the story is to provide interesting material for adult readers. It should be read as a story; the element of pleasure should be present. Because of the second grade reading level, students should be able to read the story on their own.

The first page of each chapter has a gray band at the top. This makes it easy to find the story pages. Students should be encouraged to return to these pages often and to reread the stories.

Comprehension Questions

Ten multiple-choice comprehension questions follow each chapter. There are two questions for each of these five comprehension skills:

A. Recognizing Words in Context
B. Recalling Facts
C. Keeping Events in Order
D. Making Inferences
E. Understanding Main Ideas

The letters *A* through *E* appear in the text as labels to identify the questions.

The comprehension questions are constructed to cover all parts of the chapter evenly and to bring out important points in the story. This insures that the student understands the story so far before going on to the next chapter.

Students should answer the questions immediately after reading the chapter and correct their answers using the key at the back of the book. Students should circle incorrect responses and check off correct ones.

The graphs at the back of the book help the

instructor keep track of each student's comprehension progress. The *Comprehension Progress Graph* shows comprehension percentage scores. The *Skills Profile Graph* identifies areas of comprehension weakness needing special attention and extra practice.

Language Skills

These sections cover many aspects of language study: phonics, word attack skills, simple grammar, and correct usage. The readability of these sections is higher than that of the chapters. The readability level varies depending on the vocabulary load of the specific language skill being taught.

Because the language skills are taught in clear and simple terms, most students will be able to work these sections independently. However, the instructor should be alert for opportunities to explain and further illustrate the content of the lessons.

The lessons contain exercises which give students the opportunity to practice the language skills being taught. An answer key at the back of the book makes it possible for students to correct their work.

Understanding Life Skills

Every chapter is accompanied by two sections which deal with life skills. The first, "Understanding Life Skills," introduces and fully explains a specific life skill. The life skills all revolve around some detail of modern adult life.

Because this section stresses *understanding* a certain life skill, the reading level is higher than the reading level of the story. However, the life skill lessons are presented in carefully prepared steps, and most students should be able to read and comprehend them without too much difficulty.

Questions used in the lessons are designed to focus the students' attention and to reinforce the learning. Answers for all questions are provided at the back of the book.

Applying Life Skills

Because modern-day living requires both *knowing* and *doing*, two life skills sections follow each chapter to emphasize both aspects. The second, "Applying Life Skills," is primarily a practical exercise.

This section builds on the understanding generated in the previous section. Students should be able to complete the exercise successfully by applying what they have just read.

Completing this section allows students to demonstrate their mastery of a specific life skill. It gives them the firsthand experience they need with tasks they are likely to encounter in everyday living.

An Answer Key at the back of the book helps students correct their work and gives them immediate feedback.

All units in each book are structured alike, each consisting of the six sections described here. Students quickly discover the regular pattern and are able to work with success and confidence throughout the text.

Use in Small-Group or Class Situations

Although the books in the Adult Learner Series were designed primarily for use on an individual basis, they can be used successfully in small-group or class situations. The comprehension, language and life skills questions can be adapted to whole-class instruction; this may be especially useful for students of English as a Second Language. If several students have read the stories, a group discussion may prove rewarding as well as motivating.

Writing Assignments

The comprehension questions and answers may also serve as suggestions for writing assignments.

For many students at this level, a writing assignment must be introduced in a very structured manner; otherwise, some students may find themselves unable to get started. On a group basis, the writing assignment may grow naturally out of the class discussion. In this case, the discussion may be all the introduction necessary.

On an individual basis, however, and also often within a group situation, it will be necessary to provide the student with a more concrete starting point. The teacher may find it necessary to provide model sentences or paragraphs, or to supply sentence beginnings ("If I had been there, I would have . . .") for the student to complete. The students can use their copies of the stories to search for word spellings, or the teacher may wish to write suggested words on the blackboard or provide a prepared list.

The Word List

Every word used in the story is included in the Word List, given alphabetically under the chapter in which it is first introduced. New forms that are made by adding the suffixes *-s*, *-ed*, *-ing*, and *-ly* to words that have already been introduced are indented.

The instructor may wish to scan the Word List to choose preview words in addition to the twenty in the Preview Words section at the beginning of each chapter. Non-phonetic words, which may present some difficulties in decoding, are printed in italics for quick identification.

The Word List may also be used for the study of common sight words. Since an effort has been made to provide adequate repetition of each word, most of these words should be a solid part of the student's sight vocabulary by the time he or she has finished reading the story.

Summary of the Chapters in Dr. Valdez

Chapter 1: Dr. Valdez *(Level 2.4)*

Ron Wells, a professional troubleshooter, receives a letter from a scientist, Dr. Valdez, who wants him to test a new invention. Curious, Ron goes to Dr. Valdez's lab, where he finds out that the new invention is a time machine. Dr. Valdez shows him some things that the time machine booth has brought back: a dinosaur egg shell and a piece of newspaper from the future. Ron doesn't believe that the time machine works, but he promises to return for a demonstration.

Chapter 2: The Time Machine *(Level 2.2)*

Ron returns to the lab the next day. Dr. Valdez tells him more about the time machine and shows him the adjustments for the differences in ground level over the years. He makes a demonstration run; the time machine booth returns with a pile of tiny ears of corn, placed there by prehistoric Indians. Ron is convinced and agrees to test the machine.

Chapter 3: Into the Past *(Level 1.7)*

The next day, Ron arrives for the first test. Dr. Valdez tells him that he is to go back to the age of the dinosaurs and bring back some leaves from a now-extinct tree. Ron steps into the booth, and a moment later he is 100,000,000 years in the past. He walks to a distant grove of trees and cuts two leaves. He is carried away by a flying dinosaur; when he escapes, he realizes that he is lost.

Chapter 4: Lost in the Past *(Level 1.6)*

Ron searches for the path he had made through the tall grass. Two dinosaurs fight near him. The victor leaves, and Ron climbs up on the body of the supposedly dead dinosaur to look around. Ron finds himself sitting astride its head when it suddenly lurches to its feet. Ron discovers that he can steer the dinosaur, and he locates the booth. He vows not to lose the booth again, but he feels obligated to bring something back to Dr. Valdez. Ron finds a dinosaur egg and returns with it to the lab.

Chapter 5: 2481 *(Level 1.3)*

Ron is sent into the future. Or arrival, he falls in the dark. He finds out that he had fallen into a huge cellar hole, where huge self-propelled machines are working. He meets Jit, the only human worker, who shows him around the city of 2481. Ron sees things like vast buildings surrounded by parks, moving sidewalks and flying cars. When they return to the cellar hole, the time machine booth is gone.

Chapter 6: The Man from the Future *(Level 1.8)*

Ron tells Jit that he needs the booth to return to

1981. Jit suggests that Ron use a modern time machine, but explains that he will have to know his coordinates, pass a test, raise money—and wait. Ron feels forlorn, but then the machines return the booth. Ron spends two happy days sightseeing, then frets as he waits for the new building to be raised to the right level for his return. An even larger machine helps out; Ron bids farewell to Jit and returns to a frantic Dr. Valdez. Fascinated by his story, Dr. Valdez wants Ron to make further tests, but Ron goes home.

Words Introduced in the Story

Non-phonetic words are in italics. New forms of words already introduced are indented.

Chapter 1: Dr. Valdez

a
about
afraid
after
again
against
air
all
almost
alone
always
am
an
and
another
any
anyone
anything
are

around
as
asked
at

back
bad
be
because
been
before
began
believe
bent
bet
better
big
    bigger

bills
bit
blow
    blows
blown
booth
bottom
bring
but
by

cage
call
    called
came
can
can't
carefully

carried
case
chance
change
city
climbed
clock
cold
come
control
controls
costs
could
couldn't
course
crazy
cut

danger
dangerous
day
  days
dear
deck
deep
dials
did
didn't
dinosaur
  dinosaurs
do
doing
does
doesn't
done
don't
door
down

Dr.
drove

egg
else
end
even
everyone
eyes

fake
fast
feel
  feels
feet
felt
few
find
first
fix
floor
for
Ford
friend
from
front
full
fun
funny
future

gave
get
  getting
give
glad
go
  going
gone
good
got
great
ground
guy

had
hadn't
hair
hall
hand
  hands
happen
hard
hated
have
haven't
he
head
help
here
hey
hide
him
himself
his
history
hold
home
hopefully
house
how
hum
hurry
  hurried
hurt

I
I'd
if
I'll
I'm
in
into
invented
is
isn't
it
it's
itself

Jeep
job
  jobs
just

keep
kept
key
killed
kind
know
  knows

lab
last
lay
leaned
led
left
leg
letter
  letters
life
like
limp
lived
living
lock
lonely
long
look
  looked
  looking
  looks
lot
loud

machine
  machines
mad
mail
make
man
  man's
may
maybe
me
means
might
mine
minute
money
monkey
more
morning
most
mother
  mother's
Mr.
much
must
my

named
need
  needed
never
new
newspaper
  newspapers
next
nice
no
not
nothing
now
number

of
oh
OK
old
on
one
open
  opened
or
other
our
out
over

paper
parked
  parking
part
past
people
person
phone
picked

pile
place
pockets
pointed
power
proof
pushed
put

quickly
quietly
quite

ran
rang
read
ready
real
  really
rest
right
rocky
Ron
room
run
  running
runners

sadly
safely
said
same
sat
saw
say
  saying
scientist
  scientist's

secret
see
seemed
sent
set
shake
shell
shook
shoot
short
show
side
sit
slot
slowly
small
smile
  smiled
smooth
so
some
someone
something
sometimes
somewhere
sounded
stand
start
  started
  starting
stay
step
  stepped
still
stood
stopped
strange
strong

stuck
studies
suddenly
sure
switch
  switches

take
  takes
talk
  talking
tell
  telling
test
  tested
than
thank
that
that's
the
them
then
there
these
they
thin
thing
  things
think
  thinking
this
thought
through
till
time
tired
to
today

told
tomorrow
too
took
touched
travel
trip
turn
  turned

under
unlocked
up
use

Valdez
very

wait
  waiting
walk
  walked
  walking

wall
want
  wanted
was
wasn't
waste
watching
way
we
weeks
well
  Wells
went
were
what
what's
when
where
while
white
who
why
will
wind

wires
with
won't
word
work
  worked
  working
  works
worry
worse
would
wouldn't
writing

year
  years
yes
yet
you
your
you've
yours

Chapter 2: The Time Machine

across
ago
along
anywhere
arm
  asking
away

B.C.
  being
bed
  believed

blurred
burned
button

calm
circles
closely
clothes
  comes
corn

deal

different
dig
  digging
dried
dropped
dug

ear
ears
easy
eat
everything

fall
far
filled
flashed
forget
found
free

glowed
goes
grabbed
grow

hang
happened
happily
headed
hearing
held
holding
hole
houses
humming

inches
Indian
Indians
inside
I've

July
jumped

knew
known

later
lean
less
let
let's
letting
level
light
lights
line
lit
louder
loudly
lower

matter
mean
mind
minutes
moment
move
moved
moves

off
only
onto
outside

P.M.
pocket
pulled

questions

red
Ron's

same
second
seem
send
shaking
she's
should
shouted
showed
shut
signed
sitting
snapped
softly
soon
sound
space
spend
split
spot
standing
stayed
sticking
store
studied
sunk

tests
their
there's
those
threw
throw
times
tiny
top
true
turning
two

used
using

warms
watch
watched

waved
weakly
wild
winter
woke
wonder

worried
wrong

you're
yourself

Chapter 3: Into the Past

above
already
aren't
arms
asks

banged
beating
between
bird
bits
black
blade
boat
body
boy
breath
broke

care
cave
catch
check
checked
claws
climbing
closed
closer
coffee

coming
count
country
crack
cry
cup
cutting

damp
dial
died
dragging
drink
dropping

each
eaten
enough

falling
faster
fell
fern
ferns
fight
five
flap
flapped
flat

fool
footsteps

given
grass
guess
guessed

hacked
hacking
handle
happy
harder
hardly
hear
here's
he's
hidden
high
hit
hoping
hot
hour
hours
huge

idea
inch
its

jungle

knife
knock
knocked

land
late
leaves
legs
lift
lifted
little
locked
lost
low
lowest

meant
middle
mile
mountains
mouth
moving

near
nearly
neck
night

ones

path
pet
pictures
plants
plate
popped
pot
pretty
pull

quiet

rain
raining
rainy
rats
reach
reached
reaching
remember
ripped
rushed

shadow
shining
skin
slid
slipped
slow
somehow
sounds
splashing
spotted
street
stump
sun
swamp
swamps
swing
swung

table
tail
tall
teeth
ten
testing
tree
trees
trunk
try
tried

waited
warm
water
we're
wet
which
window
wings
without

you'll

Chapter 4: Lost in the Past

awake

baby
badly
bang
beside
bites
biting
bleeding

break
gun
rose

circle
close
covered
crashing
crawled
crying
cuts

dark
dead
dinosaur's
dove

ever

father
fighting
finding
fish
flew
flying
food
foot
football
four

gasps
growl
growling

hanging
heard
heave
higher
hill
hope
horn
hung

kicked
kicking
kill
killer

longer
lose
lying

marks
mess
mighty

pulling

question
quieter

riding
rocked
rolling

safe
scales
scrape
scream
seen
shade
sharper
shine
slamming
sliding
slipping
smiling
steeper
steer
stiff
story

tearing
third
three
throwing
thrown
thud
tightly
trying

waked
waking
wide

Chapter 5: 2481

anyway
August

beam
below
block
bones
box
boy
broken

building
buildings
bump
buttons

camera
camping
car
cars
cellar
children
cities
clean
clicking
coat
computer
computers
crash
crashed
crashes

dangers
dash
Doc
doctors
driving

every

factories
fishing
flashlight
floating
foods

gasped
green

heap
hop

ideas
it'll

Jit
Jit's

keeping

labs
landed
levels
lighter
live
lucky

main
meet
miles

name
names
nearer
neatly

offices

pack
packed
park
parks
parts
pat
patting
picture
piled

places
plans
pointing
pools
proudly
putting

ride
roads

safer
sail
scared
school
schools
seats
shined
smaller
smart
smoothly
soft
sorry
steering
stores
streets
study
surprised
swimming

tape
tapes
themselves
they've
thousands
trap

unloaded

Valdez's

weren't
we've

wheel
world
wow

yard

zipped
zoomed

Chapter 6: The Man from the Future

ask

beginning
best
book
build
bus

changed
cheat
closing
counts

dragged

east

famous

gives
guy's

happening

happens

joker
jumping

leaning

nine
north
notes
numbers

office
older
once
own

page
pass
push

rid
roll

rolled
rules
runs

save
scientists
shouting
shows
sick
someday
sooner
south
stomped
supper

thanks

unlocking
upset

west
woods
write

Answer Key

Comprehension Questions

Chapter 1

1. b	2. d	3. a	4.c	5.d
6. c	7. a	8. d	9. b	10. c

Chapter 2

1. b	2. d	3. c	4. a	5. b
6. a	7. a	8. b	9. a	10. d

Chapter 3

1. b	2. d	3. a	4. c	5. b
6. c	7. d	8. d	9. d	10. c

Chapter 4

1. c	2. c	3. b	4. c	5. a
6. d	7. b	8. a	9. d	10. b

Chapter 5

1. a	2. c	3. c	4. b	5. a
6. a	7. b	8. a	9. c	10. b

Chapter 6

1. c	2. c	3. d	4. d	5. a
6. b	7. b	8. c	9. c	10. a

Language Skills

Chapter 1: Exercise 1

1. new
2. fresh
3. green
4. pretty
5. third
6. first
7. good
8. dull
9. bad
10. clever

Exercise 2

1. round 2. red 3. large 4. empty 5. hot

Exercise 3

The ~~little~~ boy walked down the ~~long, dark~~ street. It was a ~~rainy~~ night. He saw an ~~old~~, ~~empty~~ house behind some ~~dead~~ trees on the corner. The house had many ~~broken~~ windows. He saw a ~~strange~~, ~~old~~ animal look through one of them.

Chapter 2: Exercise 1

1. noisily
2. sadly
3. faithfully
4. cheerfully
5. slowly
6. prettily
7. quietly
8. nervously
9. smoothly
10. fearfully

Exercise 2

1. clearly
2. carefully
3. seriously
4. lightly
5. silently

Exercise 3

Tim looked ~~playfully~~ at Pat. She sat ~~calmly~~ reading a book. She ~~clearly~~ did not see him. He watched her ~~cheerfully~~, waiting for her to look up She read on ~~steadily~~. ~~Slowly~~ and ~~quietly~~ Tim rose from his chair. He walked ~~silently~~ across the room to where Pat was sitting. He stopped ~~carefully~~ in back of her chair. ~~Suddenly~~ he took her book and said ~~loudly~~, "Surprise!"

Chapter 3: Exercise 1

1. faster
2. shorter
3. greener
4. softer
5. taller
6. lighter

Exercise 2

1. quieter
2. nicer
3. wiser
4. shorter
5. cleaner
6. smaller
7. wider
8. whiter
9. sweeter
10. tighter

Exercise 3

1. luckier
2. trickier
3. noisier
4. dirtier
5. crazier

Exercise 4

1. younger
2. funnier
3. higher
4. brighter
5. faster
6. easier
7. sweeter
8. looser
9. cuter
10. narrower

Chapter 4: Exercise 1

1. 4 more valuable
2. 4 more mysterious
3. 4 more intelligent
4. 3 more disgusting
5. 3 more expensive

Exercise 2

1. more serious
2. more wonderful
3. brighter
4. wilder
5. more frightened
6. more unusual
7. harder
8. more terrible
9. meaner
10. cooler

Exercise 3

1. more quickly
2. more carefully
3. more happily
4. more quietly
5. more easily
6. more smoothly
7. more clearly
8. more bravely
9. more steadily
10. more honestly

Chapter 5: Exercise 1

1. newest
2. thickest
3. nearest
4. youngest
5. strongest
6. wildest

Exercise 2

1. poorest
2. darkest
3. boldest
4. sharpest
5. fairest

Exercise 3

1. ripest
2. finest
3. densest
4. simplest
5. bluest

Exercise 4

1. tastiest
2. fluffiest
3. shiniest
4. shadiest
5. chilliest

Exercise 5

1. sunniest
2. cheapest
3. neatest
4. brightest
5. richest
6. safest
7. tiniest
8. tamest
9. weakest
10. bumpiest

Chapter 6: Exercise 1

1. 3 most disgusting
2. 3 most talented
3. 3 most comfortable
4. 3 most plentiful
5. 4 most dependable
6. 3 most colorful

Exercise 2

1. clearest
2. most reliable
3. most enormous
4. swiftest
5. warmest
6. most elegant
7. kindest
8. most inexpensive
9. most depressing
10. dullest

Exercise 3

1. most secretly
2. most gladly
3. most slowly
4. most quietly
5. most loudly

Exercise 4

1. most gracefully
2. most seriously
3. most steadily
4. most lightly
5. most crossly
6. most nervously
7. most cheerfully

Understanding Life Skills

Chapter 1

1. Yes
2. Yes
3. Bush Ends His GOP Race
4. Yes
5. No
6. An explanation of what is in a photograph
7. 6

Chapter 2

1. No
2. a. news
   b. editorial
3. Yes
4. Yes
5. New York
6. Detroit

Chapter 3

1. 2
2. 9
3. 1
4. 6

Chapter 4

1. FORT WAYNE
2. May 29

Chapter 5

1. 1979
2. a. 44,000
   b. mi.

Chapter 6

1. 4
2. Little House on the Prairie
3. 25
4. House Calls
5. Red Sox

Chapter 1: Exercise 1

1. 4
2. 4
3. 5
4. The President Is Shocked
5. Tree limbs covered with ash
6. There'll Be Gas

Exercise 2

1. Dodgers Down By 1
2. Storm Watch For South County
3. Tax Break For Elderly
4. Bus Fares Go Up Next Month

Exercise 3

1. 7
2. BUDGET

Chapter 2: Exercise 1

1. Sports
2. News
3. Editorials
4. Amusements
5. News
6. Sports

Exercise 2

1. Kansas City
2. 24
3. 21
4. Minnesota
5. 18

Chapter 3

1. 3
2. a. B-1
   b. C-10
   c. C-1
   d. B-6
   e. C-7
   f. C-6
   g. A-1
   h. A-10
   i. B-8
   j. A-8

Chapter 4: Exercise 1

1. Fire
2. MONTREAL

Exercise 2

1. Who?
2. What?
3. When?
4. Where?

Chapter 5: Exercise 1

1. FORD MUSTANG
2. 1968
3. Like new.
4. $700
5. firm

Exercise 2

1. OAKLAND
2. a. Pine
   b. St.
3. a bdrm.
   b. apt.

Chapter 6

1. a. 6:00 P.M.
   b. 6:30 P.M.
2. 6
3. Elephants
4. Salad
5. a. Channel 6
   b. Channel 7

Comprehension Progress Graph

How to Use the Comprehension Progress Graph

1. At the top of the graph, find the number of the chapter you have just read.
2. Follow the line down until it crosses the line for the number of questions you got right.
3. Put a dot • where the lines cross.
4. The numbers on the other side of the graph show your comprehension score.

For example, this graph shows the score of a student who answered 7 questions right for Chapter 1. The score is 70%. →

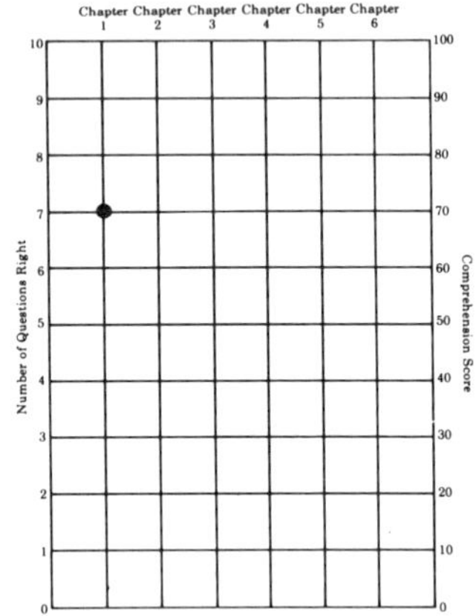

This same student got scores of 80% and 90% on Chapters 2 and 3. The line connecting the dots keeps going up. This shows that the student is doing well. ←

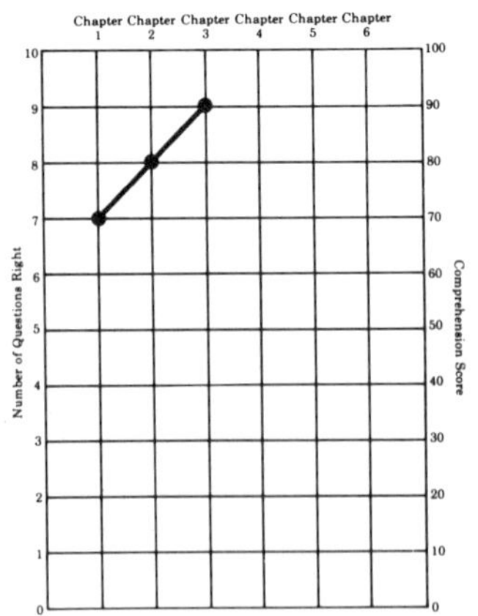

If the line between the dots on your graph does not go up, or if it goes down, see your instructor for help.

Comprehension Progress

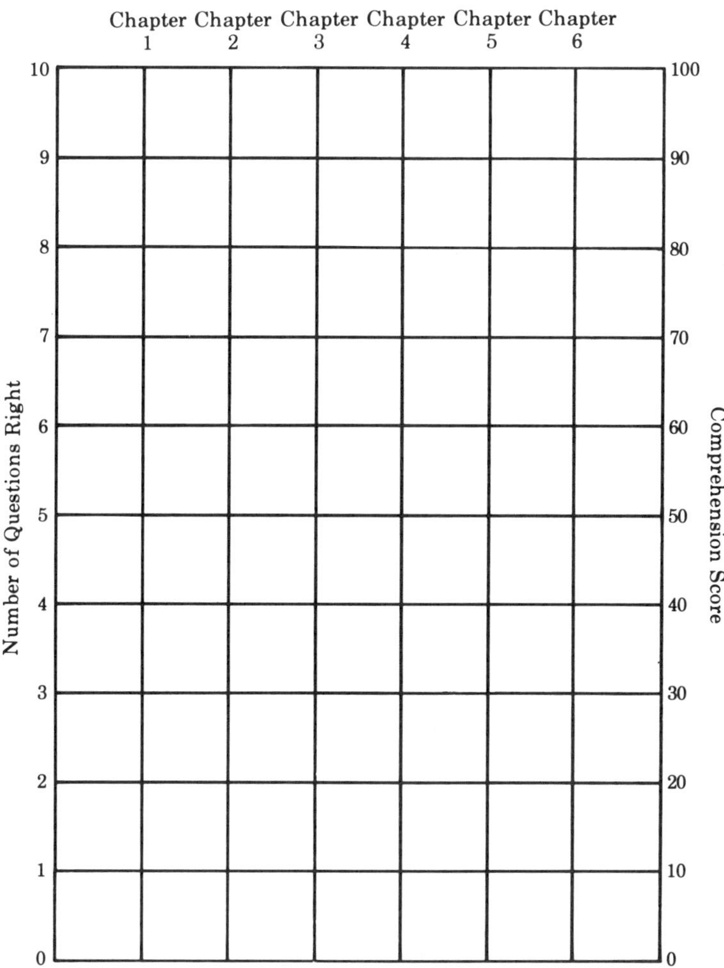

Skills Profile Graph

How to Use the Skills Profile Graph

1. There is a block on this graph for every comprehension question in the book.
2. Every time you get a question wrong, fill in a block which has the same letter as the question you got wrong. For example, if you get an A question wrong, fill in a block in the A row. Use the right row for each letter.

Look at the graph. It shows the profile of a student who got 3 questions wrong. This student got an A question wrong, a C question wrong, and a D question wrong.

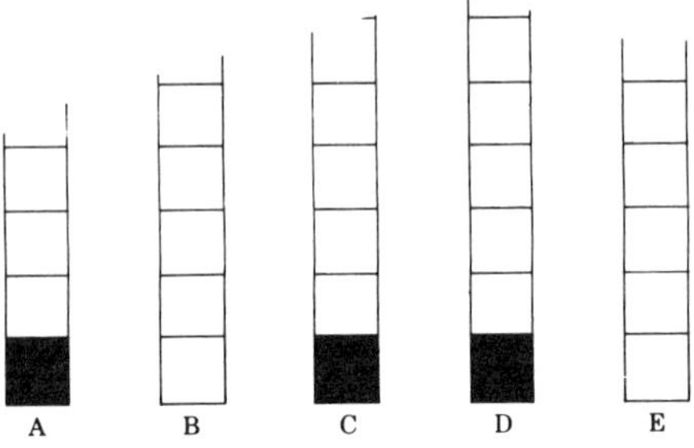

On the next chapter, this same student got 4 questions wrong and has filled in 4 more blocks.

The graph now looks like this. This student seems to be having trouble on question C. This shows a reading skill that needs to be worked on.

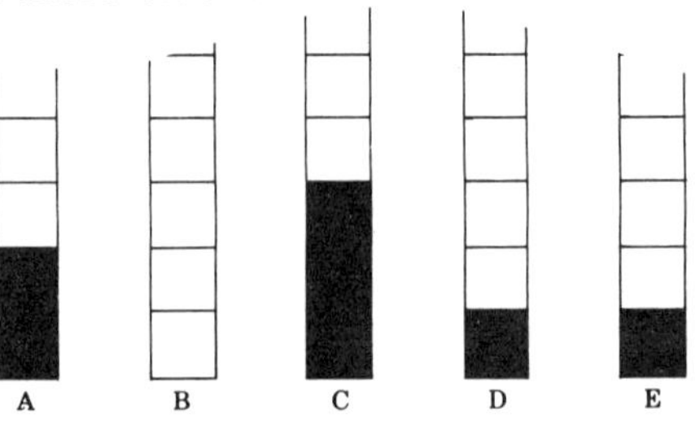

The blocks that are filled in on your graph tell you and your instructor the kinds of questions that give you trouble.

Look for the rows that have the most blocks filled in. These rows will be higher than the others. Talk to your instructor about them. Your instructor may want to give you extra help on these skills.

Skills Profile

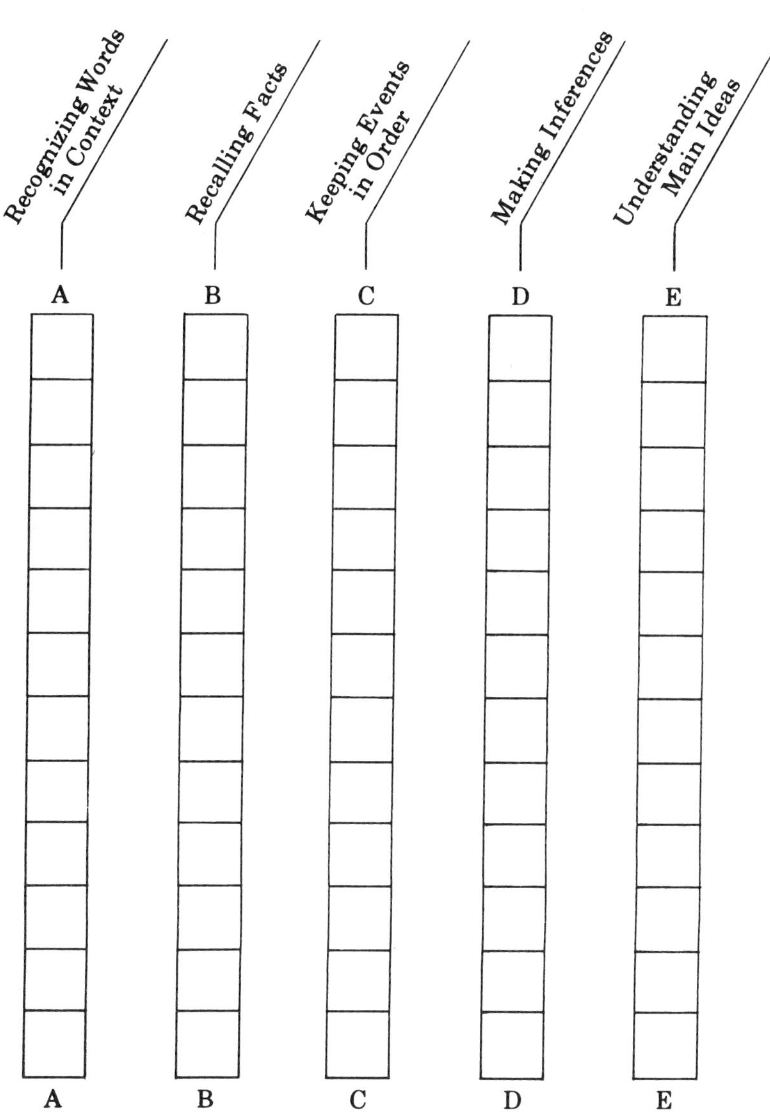